MW00424589

Regeneration

Regeneration

Made New by the Spirit of God

Banner Mini-Guides
Key Truths

David B. McWilliams

THE BANNER OF TRUTH TRUST

THE BANNER OF TRUTH TRUST

Head Office
3 Murrayfield Road
Edinburgh, EH12 6EL
UK

North America Office
PO Box 621
Carlisle, PA 17013
USA

banneroftruth.org

© The Banner of Truth Trust, 2020

ISBN
Print: 978 1 84871 971 2
EPUB: 978 1 84871 972 9
Kindle: 978 1 84871 973 6

*

Typeset in 10/14 pt Minion Pro
at the Banner of Truth Trust, Edinburgh

Printed in the USA by
Versa Press, Inc.,
East Peoria, IL

For

EVAN McWILLIAMS

my only son
with love and respect
2 Timothy 3:14, 15

Contents

Introduction

'You must be born again' (John 3:7). These words spoken by Jesus to Nicodemus, a prominent Jewish leader, are very important. After all, Jesus told him plainly that he could not enter God's kingdom without the new birth. If we do not believe in Christ we need to understand these words because they are vital to salvation. But, even if we are believers already, exploring these words opens up to us a rich mine of truth about God's salvation that each of us needs. By investigating the words 'you must be born again' Christians come to realize that salvation is far greater than we could possibly have imagined.

There is one big question behind all this: is salvation of the Lord, alone, or is it partly of man? This was the monumental issue confronted by the Protestant Reformers in the sixteenth century. It was the issue at the heart of their life-and-death contest with the Roman Catholic Church concerning the Bible's teaching on justification—that is, what it means to be accepted by God. The Roman Church insisted that our works play a role in this, but, the Reformers declared boldly from the Bible, and particularly from the letters of the apostle Paul, that the righteousness we need for acceptance with God is credited to us by grace and received by faith alone. Sinners contribute nothing to their acceptance with God. The lost and ruined sinner can do nothing to merit justification; Christ has done it all. And these debates were not just heady, inconsequential discussions; rather, they were matters of the greatest weight, matters of eternity.

Justification is a declaration in God's court of law that comes from outside of us. It is a once-for-all juridical (legal) act. However, salvation is a matter not only of what God declares regarding us, but also of what he has done within us. Our Saviour came to deal the death blow not only to the guilt of our sin, but also to the power of sin in our lives. The new birth, or 'regeneration,' as it is more technically called, imparts life, initiating real spiritual growth and ongoing change in our lives. This new life is preserved by God's grace until the believer is finally glorified. Reformed theology (which has its roots in the faithful Bible preaching of the Protestant Reformation) has stressed not only the legal side of salvation, but also the regenerating and renovating side of the gospel message.

After the Reformation, the Synod of Dordt (1618–19), an assembly of Reformed leaders from many churches with a Reformation heritage, met to answer the claims about salvation put forward by Jacob Arminius. He and his followers had insisted that man contributes to his salvation. His viewpoint remains, in various forms, popular today. The basic idea in this teaching is that the Holy Spirit's role in salvation is one of persuading a sinner to believe, but it is up to man's free will to decide whether or not to begin and continue in the Christian life. The Synod of Dordt firmly concluded that the Arminian teaching was out of step with the teaching of the Bible. Historical circumstances raised vital questions, but the Bible supplied the answers.

This issue has cropped up repeatedly in the history of the church, showing how vital it is to understand what the Bible says about it. And that is what we will explore together in this little book: the biblical doctrine of the new birth brought about in God's sovereign grace for those who 'were born, not of blood nor of the will of the flesh nor of the will of man, but of God' (John 1:13).

4/2/22 REFORMED THEOLOGY (WHICH HAS ITS ROOTS IN THE FAITHFUL BIBLE PREACHING OF THE PROTESTANT REFORMATION) HAS STRESSED NOT ONLY THE LEGAL SIDE OF SALVATION, BUT ALSO THE REGENERATING -N- RENOVATING SIDE OF THE GOSPEL MESSAGE -

1

Why We Need the New Birth
John 3:1-13

Probably there is little upon which professing Christians are more agreed than the necessity of regeneration. All agree that Jesus' teaching 'you must be born again' is indispensable. However, there is little upon which professing Christians disagree more than precisely what this new birth means. Do we ourselves decide to be regenerated? Is the new birth the direct work of the Holy Spirit in a person's soul, or does a sinner cooperate? Without that cooperation, can a sinner be born again? How does the new birth relate to our minds, hearts, wills and affections (the deepest longings of the heart)? Is baptism necessary for regeneration? Can infants be born again? When one is regenerated, must that lead to conversion and sanctification? Can regeneration be lost or is it, by its very nature, impossible to lose? These and other questions are at the heart of disagreements about regeneration.

Thankfully, God has given us his word, to which we turn for answers. In these opening chapters we will look briefly at the classic text in the Gospels about regeneration, John 3:1–13, and also at a classic text in Paul's writings on regeneration, Ephesians 2:1ff. From these texts we will explore the main thoughts that should control our understanding of this vital theme.

A learned Pharisee named Nicodemus came to Jesus under cover of night. Perhaps he was so filled with his own self-importance that he did not want to be seen talking with Jesus about the needs of his soul. As a Pharisee, Nicodemus held correct opinions about many things. He believed in the resurrection on the Day of Judgment, for example. He was very orthodox. However, even though – to use Jesus' metaphor (Matt. 23:27) – 'the outside of the cup' was clean, the heart was not. Morally, Nicodemus was unwashed and unclean.

Nicodemus seemed to flatter Jesus: 'Rabbi, we know that you are a teacher come from God, for no one can do these signs that you do unless God is with him' (3:2). Sweeping away this flattery, Jesus immediately points Nicodemus to his true need: 'Truly, truly, I say to you, unless one is born again he cannot see the kingdom of God' (3:3). The word 'again' in 'born again' is sometimes translated 'above.' The dialogue makes clear that, in this instance, Jesus is teaching what it means to be 'born again.'

Nicodemus did not understand. 'How can a man be born when he is old? Can he enter a second time into his mother's womb and be born?' (3:4). Throughout the conversation, Jesus does not let up on the necessity of a radical change of nature, the new birth. Jesus answered:

Truly, truly I say to you, unless one is born of water and the Spirit, he cannot enter the kingdom of God. That which is born of the flesh is flesh, and that which is born of the Spirit is spirit. Do not marvel that I said to you, 'You must be born again.' The wind blows where it wishes, and you hear its sound, but you do not know where it comes from or where it goes. So it is with everyone who is born of the Spirit (3:5–8).

From Jesus' answer we can see that the new birth is absolutely necessary; it is indispensable for those who would enter God's kingdom. The door of heaven is barred shut against every unregenerate person. Moreover, if it was necessary for a teacher of Israel to have this new birth, then surely it is necessary for us as well. In these verses our Lord describes the universal necessity of a radical and real change of nature.

The necessity of regeneration

What reasons does Jesus put forward to show that regeneration is universally necessary?

First, Jesus teaches that the new birth is necessary because 'that which is born of the flesh is flesh' (3:6). 'Flesh' is used in many ways in Scripture, but here it clearly means our fallen nature, depravity and sinfulness. For example, 'flesh' is used similarly in John 6:63: 'It is the Spirit who gives life; the flesh is no help at all.' It is common for older theologians to say that 'flesh cannot rise above flesh,' which ties in with Jesus' teaching here. 'Flesh' speaks of our total corruption that makes it impossible for us to see God's kingdom apart from the new birth. David put it this way in one of his most beloved psalms: 'Behold, I was brought forth in iniquity, and in sin did my mother conceive me' (Psa. 51:5). We are sinners from conception. All who are descended from Adam are born in sin; hence the necessity of the new birth.

Second, the new birth is necessary because without it we 'cannot see the kingdom of God' (3:3). Jesus is not referring to our physical eyes but to the eyes of the soul. We cannot receive, encounter, experience or be a part of God's kingdom without being enabled by regeneration. Regeneration is necessary if we are to partake in the kingdom of God. No entry into the kingdom of heaven without regeneration? Do not miss the practical impact, the eternal weight, of the new birth!

Third, regeneration is necessary to dispel our spiritual darkness. Nicodemus asks, 'How can a man be born when he is old?' (3:4). Clearly, Nicodemus is totally in the dark regarding the new birth. In his darkness he asks, 'How can these things be?' (3:9). He was a teacher in Israel but he did not understand these things. The Psalms which he read and which he could probably quote from memory were written down under God's inspiration by men who were truly God's instruments, but Nicodemus did not understand these things! What does this say to us? It tells us that, by nature, we lack real spiritual understanding until the Holy Spirit enlightens our minds in the new birth. By nature, man's mind is incapable of perceiving the splendour of Christ. This has nothing to do with intelligence. Rather, before the Holy Spirit comes to indwell us, we cannot see (Rom. 8:7–8; 1 Cor. 2:14). The purpose and direction of our minds must be changed. Only the Holy Spirit can do this, by granting the new birth.

Fourth, the new birth is necessary because fallen people are powerless to recover themselves from their fallen estate. No sinner can bring himself to new birth any more than he could bring himself to natural birth. Sinners in and of themselves are powerless to enter the kingdom of God. Despite much teaching that suggests otherwise, turning to Christ and entering the kingdom is not in our hands. Our minds and wills are corrupted by sin, so we 'cannot see the kingdom of God' (3:3, 5), we cannot rise above nature (3:6), and, so, we cannot regenerate ourselves. Any teaching that weakens the Bible's teaching about man's fallen nature, or suggests that he is not 'that depraved' or 'so fallen' and that his will is able to respond to the gospel message apart from the new birth, is out of step with Scripture. Such man-centred teaching endangers the souls of those who hear it. As we shall see later, sinners are so devastated by the corruption of the fall that every faculty of their minds, hearts, souls and wills is thoroughly depraved. Therefore, no sinner apart from the new birth can do spiritual good. The sinner is, in himself, completely impotent, powerless to redeem himself or even to place himself into a redeemable state. Hence, sinners do not seek God apart from the regenerating work of God's Spirit (Rom. 3:11), and man's sinful will is enslaved and determined to sin unless and until it is transformed by grace.

However, though man does not seek God, God does seek man. Let us notice something essential about Jesus' evangelism. In this providentially arranged meeting with Nicodemus, Jesus, the one who came to seek and save the lost, takes the opportunity to move Nicodemus to the point of distress. 'What can this mean?' 'I do not understand.' 'What are you teaching?' These questions are typical when the Holy Spirit draws sinners to Christ. Distress and sometimes total distraction often precede renewal of the heart. Perhaps you, as you read this now, have been distressed by the demand of the new birth. You are distressed by your lost condition. Biblical evangelism does not say, 'Well, when you think you are born again, then we will talk about being born again. There is no use talking about being born again since you are incapable of producing it.' No; Jesus' evangelism is the model for our own. Jesus carefully, clearly, places before Nicodemus the one thing needful and directs him to saving faith (John 3:16ff.). This is the important takeaway for evangelism: the power of the Holy Spirit accompanies the word proclaimed. While biblical evangelism is not formulaic, and there is much mystery about how a soul is brought to Christ, this one thing must always be kept front and centre: word and Spirit are not at odds, but the Spirit who inspired the word uses it in saving the lost. The minister may preach in a cemetery, as did Ezekiel the prophet in the Old Testament, but the Spirit of God can accompany that word and bring life from the dead (Ezek. 37:1ff.). So Jesus evangelizes Nicodemus. He smokes him out of every refuge bar one – Jesus himself. By urgent proclamation, seeking the lost, wooing the sinner, Jesus teaches us that 'he that winneth souls is wise' (Prov. 11:30, KJV).

The more the light dawns in your soul, the more all this will seem marvellous. The more your heart is directed to the Lamb of God, the more the world (that is, this present age under the dominion of the evil one) will lose its charms. The Spirit of God alone can break the hold of sin and the world on our lives. And when he does so, our hearts are at peace.

2

What Is the New Birth?
John 3:1-13

One of the best and most comprehensive summaries of the Bible's teaching was drawn up by the Assembly that met in Westminster from 1643 to 1653. Its Larger Catechism (Q&A 25) states that the sinner is

> utterly indisposed, disabled, and made opposite unto all that is spiritually good, and wholly inclined to all evil, and that continually.

Without the new birth, none of this can change. Does John chapter 3 help us to understand what is involved in the new birth? Indeed it does.

First, the new birth is the result of the Holy Spirit's work. 'The wind blows where it wishes, and you hear its sound, but you do not know where it comes from or where it goes. So it is with everyone who is born of the Spirit' (3:8). The danger of 'decisional regeneration,' the view that regeneration depends upon the decision of the sinner, is that it can cause sinners to think that they are somehow qualified to come to Christ, or have power to bring themselves to God. We have no qualifications and it is dangerous in evangelism to encourage people to think that they can contribute to their salvation. As the Reformed theologian Stephen Charnock put it, 'The chief design of the gospel is to beat down all glorying in ourselves.'[1]

Typically, the argument raised against this is the claim that 'God would not require a sinner to perform what he cannot do.' But, the Bible teaches that very thing. Man is responsible even though incapable. Human responsibility is a core biblical truth, but the notion that a sinner is able to turn himself is not a biblical truth. Regeneration is all of grace, from first to last. It is from God to us. The analogy of birth demands this. Moreover, it is mysterious. No matter how much we may understand about natural conception and birth, it is still mysterious. As the preacher in the Old Testament book of Ecclesiastes wrote: 'As you do not know the way the spirit comes to the bones in the womb of a woman with child, so you do not know the work of God who makes everything' (Eccles. 11:5). This sense of mystery certainly applies to making sinners new by regeneration. Regeneration does not take place at the level of our consciousness. What the new-born sinner experiences are the consequences of regeneration. The sinner becomes conscious of faith and repentance. But, the inscrutable work of the Spirit leads us on to adoration. Regeneration is, to use the words of Samuel Davies in his hymn 'Great

[1] Stephen Charnock, *The Necessity of Regeneration* (Edinburgh: Banner of Truth Trust, 2010), *Works*, vol. 3, p. 88.

God of Wonders,' 'this strange, this matchless grace, this God-like miracle of love.'

Second, regeneration is a sovereign work of the Holy Spirit. The sovereignty of God in regeneration is stressed in 3:8: 'The wind blows where it wishes, and you hear its sound, but you do not know where it comes from or where it goes. So it is with everyone who is born of the Spirit.' No one can direct the wind; it is independent. I cannot see it; I see only its results. So, too, God's regeneration is a sovereign work. It must be, since men are 'dead in … trespasses and sins' (Eph. 2:1).

Think of Christ standing before Lazarus' tomb. Jesus did not say, 'Lazarus, bring yourself to life, burst from the tomb in your own power.' Our souls are in need of that very word of the sovereign Holy Spirit that Christ spoke before Lazarus' tomb: 'come out' (John 11:43). Our hearts that are dead towards God must throb with life and vitality, the Spirit doing for us what we cannot do for ourselves (John 1:12–13). This sovereign movement of the Holy Spirit on and within our souls is all of grace. The Holy Spirit is a free agent. He is not commanded by anyone nor prohibited by anyone. Sinners are dead in sin; that is the bad news. But God is sovereign and can bring the dead to life, and that is good news. Given man's fallen estate, the sovereign regenerating work of the Spirit is the only hope for helpless sinners to enable us to respond to the gospel message – and there is not a sinner who is beyond the reach of God's free and sovereign mercy. God does not need, nor does he ask, permission to grant new life to sinners. He speaks and it is done. Those for whom Christ died must be saved and the Spirit infallibly will, as the fruit of Christ's atoning death on the cross, give life to God's chosen people and apply the gospel to our hearts. Nothing can stop him. That is good news.

Third, through regeneration the Holy Spirit cleanses the hearts of sinners. 'Unless one is born of water and Spirit, he cannot enter the kingdom of God' (3:5). This is not a reference to baptism. For one thing, Christian baptism had not yet been instituted. For another, baptism is a sign and seal of God's covenant. A sign cannot regenerate but can only point to the God who can. John 3:5 points to the work of the Holy Spirit cleansing the soul in sovereign grace. Jesus' words echo what Ezekiel prophesied long before about the fullness of salvation, which would undoubtedly have been familiar to Nicodemus: 'I will sprinkle clean water on you, and you shall be clean from all your uncleannesses, and from all your idols I will cleanse you' (Ezek. 36:25). When the Spirit regenerates us we see our foulness and we see Christ as the only fountain of cleansing.

Fourth, the new birth transforms the heart. Regeneration must be as extensive as sin. Every faculty of the human being must be renewed and real and lasting transformation begun. Our minds, affections and wills are renewed graciously by the Holy Spirit in regeneration. In John 3, Nicodemus is in darkness. He is a master in Israel but does not understand the spiritual things Jesus is teaching him. But, the promise of God in the new covenant is, 'I will give you a new heart' (Ezek. 36:26). In place of a stony heart opposed to God, the Spirit gives a heart of flesh upon which he writes God's law. When this happens the eyes of the heart are opened for the person to be able to see and enter God's kingdom. Now the truth of God can be grasped and understood. Now the light shines into the dark places of the heart and soul. Now the heart begins to be inflamed with love for God. No longer a hard-hearted sinner, through regeneration the former rebel's heart is opened and begins to love what once was hated and to understand what once was totally obscure. The affections are changed. The Holy Spirit renews and liberates the will that otherwise is bound hopelessly in the shackles of sin. Sinners who once did not want Christ now find in him their all in all. Those who once were estranged from God and his kingdom now know him and walk in his kingdom. They now want God, long for communion with God and passionately love the God they once despised.

The Puritan pastor-theologian Stephen Charnock summarizes beautifully the transformation that takes place through the new birth:

> [Regeneration] begets those for heaven, whom [Satan] had begotten for hell. It pulls down his image and sets up God's: it pulls the crown off his head, the sceptre from his hand, snatches subjects from his empire, straightens his territories, and demolishes his forts, breaks his engines, outwits his subtlety, makes his captives his conquerors, and himself the conqueror, a captive; it pulls men out of the kingdom of darkness, and translates them into a kingdom light.[1]

---

[1] Charnock, *Regeneration*, *Works*, vol. 3, p. 322.

That is the thing of beauty that God does when he regenerates a lost and needy sinner. Is this true of you? Are you born again? Do you see that without the Holy Spirit's work you cannot enter God's kingdom? Have you heard the message of Jesus in John 3, 'You must be born again'?

3

Our Need Is Greater
Than We Can Imagine
Ephesians 2:1-10

Our goal in these opening chapters is to ground our discussion of regeneration in two classic texts that capture the teaching of our Saviour and the apostle Paul on the subject. From there our study will open out to many other texts of Scripture, but we will constantly be brought back to these anchor texts. In Ephesians 2:1ff. Paul begins by spelling out the depth of human depravity and the need of sinners. Then, he ascends to the extraordinary heights of proclaiming that man's rebellion is no obstacle to God's grace. The doctrines of God, of man, and of salvation in both John 3 and Ephesians 2 contrast starkly with the teaching that is all too common today. If it seems that we are dwelling a bit too much on human sin, depravity and inability, it is because the Bible does so, because we cannot understand regeneration thoroughly without also having a thorough knowledge of sin, and because the church today is not, by and large, emphasizing these themes enough. Education is needed, not only to inform our minds but to transform our souls.

By 'regeneration' we mean that a radical, life-giving change is required in a sinner's heart so that he might enter God's kingdom. This change can only be brought about by the Spirit of God. While Jesus uses the metaphor of 'new birth' to describe this internal change, Paul uses the term 'resurrection' to describe it from a different angle.

Our misery outside of Christ

Just as Jesus, when speaking to Nicodemus, focused on the moral darkness that prevents entrance into God's kingdom, so Paul begins to explain regeneration by stressing the sinner's misery outside of Christ. He does this in three ways. Here are Paul's divinely inspired words in Ephesians. 2:1–3:

And you were dead in the trespasses and sins in which you one walked, following the course of this world, following the prince of the power of the air, the spirit that is now at work in the sons of disobedience – among whom we all once lived in the passions of our flesh, carrying out the desires of the body and the mind, and were by nature children of wrath, like the rest of mankind.

Spiritual death

Notice first, using the strongest language possible, Paul calls man's misery and inability spiritual death: 'And you were dead in the trespasses and sins in which you once walked' (2:1). Indeed, in another place Paul tells us that 'death through sin' entered the world through the fall of Adam (Rom. 5:12). The expression 'dead in trespasses and sins' makes plain that sinners are insensible to spiritual things; that, to be blunt, sinners are spiritual corpses. The Scriptures teach that our understanding of spiritual things is totally darkened (1 Cor. 2:14) and that our wills are bound in sin (John 5:40; 6:65). To speak of fallen man as spiritually dead is to say that he is powerless, totally incapable of recovering himself from his lost condition. Death cannot be made pretty. That is God's choice of metaphor as the backdrop to our need: death and inability. But, that is not all.

A rebellious walk

Paul next says that spiritually dead sinners 'walk' in rebellion and follow 'the course of this world.' For fallen sinners, spiritual death does not mean passivity as far as rebellion is concerned. On the contrary, their 'walk' leads those who do not know Christ to vile practices (Eph. 4:17–19). The manner of life of those who are spiritually dead is contrary to, and totally at odds with, the resurrection life that is found only in Christ. Do you know this? When the Spirit regenerates sinners, they come to understand that their entire lives prior to this that moment have been contrary to God's way and will.

Spiritual enslavement

Paul further insists that lost sinners are enslaved to Satan: the one they follow is 'the prince of the power of the air, the spirit that is now at work in the sons of disobedience' (2:2). Moreover, lost sinners are enslaved to their sin, what he calls 'the passions of our flesh,' and they carry out 'the desires of the body and the mind' – no part of our humanity escapes sin's influence. Its enslavement may show in drug addiction but it also may be demonstrated in what the Scottish theologian Thomas Boston called 'learned ignorance.' It may show in adultery, but also in a moral system that is focused on trying to be righteous in God's sight through our own good works. In countless ways, mental, emotional, physical, in sins of immorality, in sins of self-righteousness, man's enslavement to sin shows itself. Just as John Newton the slaver was the deepest slave of them all, so sinners, who lead others away from Christ by the 'splendid sins' of philosophy or religious practices, are the deepest slaves to sin.

Condemnation and wrath

Paul next shows that because of the fallen human heart's sinfulness, spiritual death, conformity to the vile practices of this age, and enslavement to Satan and rebellion, sinners are under God's condemnation and wrath. Indeed, he goes so far as to say we 'were by nature children of wrath, like the rest of mankind' (2:3). 'Children of wrath' means that prior to coming to Christ sinners stand condemned for their sin. Christ sacrificed himself in the place of his people, to satisfy God's justice on their behalf (Rom. 3:25). He died for sinners who must be saved from God's wrath because their sin has made them liable to that wrath (John 3:18; Psa.

7:11–13; Rom. 3:9–20; 2 Thess. 1:5–8). 'By nature children of wrath' is a terrible expression of what sin deserves. Our culture, of course, has no understanding of the depth of sin and what it deserves, but tragically the church also often fails to appreciate these matters. Unless and until we understand the monumental truths of God's holiness and wrath we will have a shallow understanding of the cross and of the utter necessity of regeneration. To say that 'the wrath of God' is upon us is to say that we are deserving of hell. Unbelief has made us cold and unresponsive to these eternal realities. We Christians are so busy with the world that we have tuned out these realities far too often. We need to bow low before the Lord and take time to contemplate the divine wrath from which Christ has rescued us.

Scripture never flatters human nature in its fallen state. The Westminster Confession of Faith (9.3) summarizes for us the paramount issues:

> Man by his fall into an estate of sin, hath wholly lost all ability of will to any spiritual good accompanying salvation: so as a natural man, being altogether averse from that good, and dead in sin, is not able, by his own strength, to convert himself, or to prepare himself thereunto.

But is there no hope for those who are spiritually dead in trespasses and sins? Let us see how Paul answers that question.

4

Salvation Is Deeper
Than We Could Imagine
Ephesians 2:1-10

Human sin is no obstacle to God's grace! As we saw in John 3, so also here in Ephesians 2, we have no ability to regenerate ourselves. Nature cannot rise above nature. But the hinge upon which Paul's argument turns is found in the words 'but God' in 2:4, from which the door swings wide open to reveal the depths of mercy and grace found in Christ:

> But God, being rich in mercy, because of the great love with which he loved us, even when we were dead in our trespasses, made us alive together with Christ – by grace you have been saved – and raised us up with him and seated us with him in the heavenly places in Christ Jesus (2:4–6).

'But God' expresses the wonder of God's sovereign intervention into the darkness and depravity of the sinner's heart.

'But God'!

We were dead in sin, 'but God'; we followed the course of this world, 'but God'; we were enslaved to Satan, 'but God'; we were under God's wrath, 'but God' has made his people alive in the risen Lord Jesus. In his rich mercy God intervened, pitying those who have broken his law. God loved his own chosen people, even 'when we were dead in our trespasses' – even, indeed, when we hated him (compare Eph. 3:17–19). When Paul speaks in verse 4 of 'the great love with which [God] loved us,' we should remember Paul's teaching on God's grace in election in Ephesians 1; that the Father

> chose us in [Christ] before the foundation of the world, that we should be holy and blameless before him. In love he predestined us for adoption as sons through Jesus Christ, according to the purpose of his will, to the praise of his glorious grace, with which he has blessed us in the Beloved (1:4–6).

Election is crucial for understanding the Bible's teaching on regeneration. Election is a joyful note in the cacophony of sin. God planned to intervene in our plight, sent his Son to the cross for our sins and draws to him those for whom Jesus shed his blood.

The fruit of God's intervention

What is the outcome of God's wondrous, sovereign, gracious and free intervention in the lives of chosen sinners described in Ephesians 2?

Spiritual resurrection and ascension

The first fruit of regeneration is spiritual resurrection and ascension. For 'even when we were dead in our trespasses' God regenerated his own: he 'made us alive together with Christ' (2:5). In part Paul means that every true believer was united to Christ, their head and representative, in his death, burial and resurrection. But the apostle also has in mind the change that takes place in those who were once 'dead' to the things of God, who 'walked' and 'followed' the ways of the world and the devil (2:1–2). The power that raises us to spiritual life is the very same divine power that raised Jesus from the dead (1:19–20). So those who once were dead in trespasses and sins have been made alive and are in vital union with the risen and ascended Christ (2:5–6) – and that for ever (2:7).

This almighty demonstration of resurrection power in the soul of spiritually dead sinners is why even the worst of sinners can be saved. This power to raise us from the dead is part and parcel of the sufficiency of the Christ preached in the Bible. What Paul describes here is not natural but gloriously supernatural. Though he misunderstood and even opposed aspects of Paul's teaching on this subject, Charles Wesley was nonetheless in line with the apostle when he wrote in his hymn 'And Can It Be?'

> Long my imprisoned spirit lay
> Fast bound in sin and nature's night;
> Thine eye diffused a quick'ning ray;
> I woke, the dungeon flamed with light;

> My chains fell off, my heart was free;
> I rose, went forth, and followed thee.

Life comes into dead spiritual limbs; the old walk of those who belonged to the old world of sin is changed into the new walk of those who belong to the new creation (2 Cor. 5:17). This means also that the regenerated sinner can now say, in the words of the Heidelberg Catechism, 'I have already now experienced in my heart the beginning of eternal joy.'[1]

The gift of saving faith

This divine intervention also results in saving faith. In the unforgettable words of the King James Version of the Bible,

> For by grace are ye saved through faith; and that not of yourselves: it is the gift of God: not of works, lest any man should boast (Eph. 2:8–9).

Salvation is all of grace, from first to last. How else could those who are spiritually dead be made alive? Grace, the source of which is God's own will and love, and the origin of which is traced back to eternity, is God's sovereign, saving movement towards chosen sinners. The initiative is always the Lord's. The resulting promise is security in Christ for ever (Eph. 1:14). But it is essential to see that the channel by which we receive this great salvation, God's gracious gift of faith, enables us to receive Christ personally.

[1] Q&A for Lord's Day 22.

Grace changes life

Then from this saving grace flows a new life that contrasts with the old, a new life of good works:

> For we are his workmanship, created in Christ Jesus for good works, which God prepared beforehand, that we should walk in them (2:10).

Grace changes people. Works that are truly good are the fruit and not the root of our relationship with God. Similarly, Paul says in Titus 2:11–14:

> For the grace of God has appeared, bringing salvation for all people, training us to renounce ungodliness and worldly passions, and to live self-controlled, upright, and godly lives in the present age, waiting for our blessed hope, the appearing of the glory of our great God and Saviour Jesus Christ, who gave himself for us to redeem us from all lawlessness and to purify for himself a people for his own possession who are zealous for good works.

This point, that the Lord raises us to a new life evidenced by good works, is often muted and denied in today's preaching. Sovereign, irresistible grace makes us new creatures (2 Cor. 5:17) and gives us new hearts by resurrection power. We are granted new affections, desires and inclinations. We now commune with God and repent of sin. The person who says: 'I can take drugs, view pornography, care nothing for God's commands, live in fornication, have no desire for Christ and his worship and people, but I remain just a carnal Christian' is not a carnal Christian. Such a person is not a Christian at all. The experience of Marion Harvie, a seventeenth-century Scottish Covenanter[1] and martyr, is an example of the transformation that accompanies regeneration. She addressed her persecutors with the 'before' and 'after' of her life. She confessed that as a young woman she had listened to the unconverted ministers forced upon the Church of Scotland but continued to live as

> a blasphemer and Sabbath-breaker, and a chapter of the Bible was a burden to me. But, since I heard this persecuted Gospel, I durst not blaspheme nor break the Sabbath, and Bible became my delight.

To which Alexander Smellie, an historian of the period, adds: 'That it had regenerated her own experience was proof sufficient that the Evangel she loved must be the authentic Word of God.'[2]

Grace for ever

Lastly, regeneration secures our souls and manifests God's grace in us for all eternity. We were suspended over hell, totally insecure, but now we who are born again are secure in grace for ever. We are raised up in union with Christ 'so that in the coming ages he might show the immeasurable riches of his grace in kindness towards us in Christ Jesus' (2:7). God did not plan our salvation to desert us.

---

[1] The Scottish Covenanters were Christians who were committed to the reformation of the church according to the word of God. Their faithfulness to Christ, the church's one and only king, offended a government who wanted to impose its own will upon the church and who treated resistance to its laws as treason.

[2] Alexander Smellie, *Men of the Covenant* (Edinburgh: Banner of Truth Trust, 1975), p. 436.

Those born again are trophies of God's saving grace and always shall be. As John Calvin said, 'It was the design of God to hallow in all ages the remembrance of so great a goodness.'[1] In the 'coming ages' God's grace will forever be seen in those he has regenerated. Christian, God has not only shown his grace to you in the past, he will continue to show his grace to you for all ages to come. 'Every word of God proves true; he is a shield to those who take refuge in him' (Prov. 30:5).

Without any contribution from us, God has brought us to life, raised us in Christ and shown the immeasurable riches of his grace. What does it take to make alive a dead sinner? It requires God's 'great might that he worked in Christ when he raised him from the dead' (1:19–20). Regeneration is not man's work but God's. In it, God seeks his own glory.

We have looked at two classic texts on regeneration. In John 3, Jesus taught Nicodemus that the new birth is indispensable. In Ephesians 2, Paul teaches that only the almighty grace of God can raise the spiritually dead to life. These texts have opened up for us avenues that we must explore in more depth, particularly answering two questions. The first is, what makes regeneration necessary? The second: how does the sovereignty of God relate to regeneration?

But, before moving on, let me stress again that if there is no evidence that you have been raised from spiritual death,

---

[1] John Calvin, *Ephesians*, in *Calvin's Commentaries* (Grand Rapids: Baker, 1979), p. 226.

then you need a power beyond yourself, beyond nature. A theologian from long ago said that lead can be shaped into many figures – a flower or a heart – but lead it remains. So it is with fallen human nature. You may try to alter yourself or improve yourself or your circumstances, but that is not the same as being born again by God's Spirit. You need a power that can transform your heart. You need the same power that raised Jesus from the dead to bring you to life.

5

Sin Is the Root of Our Problem

My eye was drawn to what was written on a church marquee in the main thoroughfare of a small town. Those travelling up the road would read: 'We bear no guilt for Adam's sin. Ezekiel 18:20.' Those coming down the road would see: 'Total hereditary depravity is not biblical.' As I reflected on these words, what disturbed me most was the thought that many members of churches whose doctrinal standards are theologically sound might nonetheless agree with those statements. Explicit teaching on 'original sin' is increasingly rare and little understood.

If one thinks that sin is a minor thing, that human depravity is not so great after all and that man by his 'free will' can become a Christian, then regeneration will be viewed as something that man can attain, or, at least, that by cooperating with God's Spirit man can put himself in a savable state. Such people think that salvation is a matter that can be left to our own decision. Since so many professing Christians would be sympathetic to the statements mentioned above, we need to pause and think about this matter more closely, because it affects our entire view of the gospel and its proclamation. It relates especially to what we have been saying already about the vital need for us to be born again if we are to enter God's kingdom. So what makes regeneration necessary? The answer is that by nature we are sinners and fallen creatures.

The fall of man

The Bible's teaching on regeneration is directly linked to the fall of man in the garden of Eden and the fact that what happened there had profound implications for the entire human race descended from Adam. (It also lies very much at the heart of how the Bible explains the relationship of Christ to his redeemed people.) The relationship between God and Adam was a covenant relationship in which Adam as the head and representative of the human race was called to obey God. Adam was commanded not to eat of the fruit from the tree of the knowledge of good and evil (Gen. 1:26–31). Now it is important for us to know that Adam was not acting in the capacity of a private individual; rather, he was the representative of the entire human race. So, when he broke the covenant God made with him, the result was that all who are naturally descended from Adam come into the world guilty and morally corrupted.

The relationship between Adam and his descendants is fundamental to our need of regeneration. Romans 5:12–21 clearly establishes the doctrine that the guilt of Adam's sin is imputed to his descendants and also that the corruption of humanity is the consequence of Adam's disobedience.

The entire human race was in Adam, its representative, and therefore, as the Westminster Shorter Catechism puts it,

> The covenant being made with Adam, not only for himself, but for his posterity; all mankind, descending from him by ordinary generation, sinned in him, and fell with him, in his first transgression (Q. 16).

Adam's breach of the first covenant is crucial for understanding the covenant of grace.

> Man, by his fall, having made himself incapable of life by that covenant, the Lord was pleased to make a second, commonly called the covenant of grace.[1]

Correctly understanding sin and the gospel depends upon understanding the historical existence of Adam and the historical fall of the human race in Adam. Note Paul's language:

> Therefore, just as sin came into the world through one man, and death through sin, and so death spread to all men because all sinned … (Rom. 5:12).

Again,

> For as by the one's man's disobedience the many were made sinners, so by the one man's obedience the many will be made righteous (5:19).

These and similar verses demand belief in an historical Adam and the fall of humanity in him. The third chapter

(

---

[1] Westminster Confession of Faith, 7.3; compare Larger Catechism, Q&A 30, 31.

of Genesis is not only about the sad and tragic rebellion of Adam, but about the fall of the entire human race in Adam. The *New England Primer* rightly and succinctly put the matter: 'in Adam's fall, we sinned all.'

Original sin

When Adam was placed in the garden, he was in fellowship with God and he lived in a state of innocence. Surrounded with incalculable bounty, Adam was forbidden one thing:

> And the LORD God commanded the man, saying, 'You may surely eat of every tree of the garden, but of the tree of the knowledge of good and evil you shall not eat, for in the day that you eat of it you shall surely die' (Gen. 2:16–17).

But Adam broke God's law (1 John 3:4). The consequence of Adam's fall was death. In Genesis 5 we read, 'When God created man, he made him *in the likeness of God*' (5:1). The contrast between Adam's original and fallen states could not be made starker when we go on to read that Adam 'fathered a son *in his own likeness, after his image*' (5:3), with the consequence for Adam's posterity, underscored in the constant refrain as his immediate descendants are listed, '… and he died.' We should not soften the meaning of the text. Death is physical, but the profound point is that man, once God's moral image-bearer, is so no longer. Indeed, since regeneration restores that moral image that consists in knowledge, righteousness and holiness (Eph. 4:24; Col. 3:10), man's death as the result of the fall means that knowledge, righteousness and holiness, as far as man's ability to restore them is concerned, were irretrievably lost and could only be restored by a sovereign work of God's grace. The Bible chronicles – and all of life demonstrates – what Paul calls our being 'dead in trespasses and sins' (Eph. 2:1). Therefore, the mournful reality is that everyone born into the world is born with a corrupt nature, depraved in the totality of its being.

'Original sin' is a term and concept that is almost forgotten in the modern church. But it is vital that it be recovered. Original sin speaks of the corruption of man's nature as the result of the fall of Adam. Scripture teaches that from the very beginning of life men come into this world sinful and corrupt. This was David's confession: 'Behold, I was brought forth in iniquity, and in sin did my mother conceive me' (Psa. 51:5). Given the criminality and guilt of Adam's rebellion, the fall of Adam has both judicial and moral elements to it. This means that the great need of the sinner is first justification: acceptance with God, which is procured by Christ's perfect obedience to the law of God and by his substitutionary death, the payment of the penalty due to the sins of his people. The imputation of the perfect righteousness of Christ justifies the sinner who receives and rests on Christ alone for salvation. Furthermore, the new birth and the subsequent progressive moral renovation of the sinner's heart and life is no less essential. These also were purchased at the high cost of the blood of Christ. In this book we are stressing the moral side of our fallen condition and its restoration by sheer grace.

As originally created, Adam was constituted righteous. He was positively righteous and by nature inclined towards righteousness. Since his fall, however, Adam and his descendants are morally corrupt. Once a beautiful palace, man is now an empty ruin. How does original sin, the corruption of our nature as a result of our fall in Adam, manifest itself? How do the Scriptures demonstrate that we are born in a state of depravity? To that theme we now turn.

6

How Damaged Are We by Sin?

Original sin is frequently denied or minimized by professing Christians and especially ministers. However, the Scriptures pervasively teach and assume the total corruption of man's nature as a consequence of the fall. Furthermore, man's fallen nature is also clearly manifested in actual sins. The Scriptures are unambiguous that every human being is born in sin. Here are some of the ways in which the Scriptures clearly teach the doctrine of original sin.

First, as already mentioned, there is the sad fact of death. Death is not 'natural' but is the most unnatural thing in the world. Death is the result of the fall of man. 'The wages of sin is death' (Rom. 6:23). Death, the result of Adam's transgression against God's law, is variously manifested:

• *Judicial death.* This means condemnation in God's court of law. Since the fall, man is by nature guilty and under God's just wrath.

• *Death of the body.* The corruption of the body and its return to dust is the result of the fall of man (Gen. 3:19; 5).

• *Death of the soul, spiritual death.* The corruption of our nature and our depravity due to sin is death (Eph. 2:1). This includes the corruption of our understanding, or our wills, affections and consciences. Man is not born a 'blank slate' but rather, in his spiritual corruption, is dead and insensible to spiritual things (1 Cor. 2:14).

• *Death at the judgment, the 'second death'* (Rev. 2:11; 20:6, 14; 21:8). The unjust shall be raised as Jesus taught in John 5:25–29. 'They shall be dragged forth like so many malefactors out of a dungeon, to be led to execution.'[1]

• *Fear*, an inseparable component of death. Fear has been a great part of death since the fall (Heb. 2:14–15).

Thank God, as the old theologians often said, that when Adam fell, he fell on Christ! Christ has freed his people from death. He has passed through the grave. He rose on the third day according to the Scriptures. Nonetheless, until a person is regenerated by the Spirit of God, he is held captive by death and is spiritually unable to hear the good news of deliverance for sinners that comes through Christ.

Second, the Scriptures teach that fallen man is 'flesh.' Jesus makes plain in John 3:6, 'That which is born of the flesh is flesh.' Here the Lord Jesus speaks of the fallen and corrupt nature of man. 'Flesh' here means fallen, lost, corrupt human nature. Paul uses the term 'flesh' in the same way on many occasions, such as in Romans 8:5–8:

> For those who live according to the flesh set their minds on the things of the flesh, but those who live according to

---

[1] Thomas Boston, *Human Nature in Its Fourfold State* (Edinburgh: Banner of Truth Trust, 2015), p. 385.

the Spirit set their minds on the things of the Spirit. For to set the mind on the flesh is death, but to set the mind on the Spirit is life and peace. For the mind that is set on the flesh is hostile to God, for it does not submit to God's law; indeed, it cannot. Those who are in the flesh cannot please God.

Just as Paul here contrasts the flesh with God's Spirit, so Jesus in his discussion with Nicodemus about the new birth makes it plain that flesh cannot rise above flesh. Men and women who are depraved by sin in the totality of their beings are incapable of life apart from the Holy Spirit's sovereign intervention. Indeed, the works of the flesh are enumerated by Paul in Galatians 5:19–21:

Now the works of the flesh are evident: sexual immorality, impurity, sensuality, idolatry, sorcery, enmity, strife, jealousy, fits of anger, rivalries, dissensions, divisions, envy, drunkenness, orgies, and things like these. I warn you, as I warned you before, that those who do such things will not inherit the kingdom of God.

Sinful humanity, apart from the new birth, is 'flesh,' sinful, debased and ruined.

Third, the Scriptures teach that man's mind and spirit are 'filthy' apart from Christ. This was not true of Adam before his fall; he was originally righteous. After the fall, Adam's descendants have hearts that are filthy and morally polluted (2 Cor. 7:1). The human heart is polluted from conception. We see this in Genesis 5:3: '[Adam] fathered a son in his own likeness.' Since the fall the Lord looks upon man outside of Christ and sees 'that every intention of the thoughts of his heart [is] only evil continually' (Gen. 6:5). Indeed, 'the intention of man's heart is evil from his youth' (Gen. 8:21). David also says, 'Behold, I was brought forth in iniquity, and in sin did my mother conceive me' (Psa. 51:5). 'Does a spring pour forth from the same opening both fresh and salt water?' (James 3:11). Indeed, of the fallen, sinful human heart, Scripture declares: 'The heart is deceitful above all things, and desperately sick; who can understand it?' (Jer. 17:9). Since the fall of the race in Adam, the human heart is filled with lust and covetousness (Rom. 7:7).

Fourth, the Scriptures describe the fallen human heart as totally depraved and corrupt. One notable example is Romans 3:9–20. In this passage Paul speaks of the universal corruption of the human race, quoting from many other places in the Scriptures, particularly the Psalms. In the first two chapters of Romans Paul has been arguing that Gentile and Jew alike are under God's wrath and in need of the gospel. In this passage Paul summarizes the theme, declaring that human depravity is universal. Having stated that 'both Jews and Greeks are under the power of sin,' Paul, citing various Old Testament passages, drives the point home: 'None is righteous, no, not one; no one … seeks God. All have turned aside; together they have become worthless; no one does good, not even one' (3:11–12). The Scriptures declare that the entire human race is 'under the power of sin.' No one is accepted. Man sins because man is a sinner; actual sins inevitably flow from corrupt hearts.

In Romans 3:9–20, Paul teaches that sin is manifested in human speech. Primarily citing the Psalms, Paul states:

> 'Their throat is an open grave; they use their tongues to deceive.' 'The venom of asps is under their lips.' 'Their mouth is full of curses and bitterness' (3:13–14).

The holy God himself makes this declaration in his own word regarding human sinfulness. It is important to notice that when Paul wishes to demonstrate the universality of sin he turns to human speech and what the Bible says about it. Hearing God's judgment upon our speech stops our mouths from boasting (3:19). 'When words are many, transgression is not lacking' (Prov. 10:19). Paul must remind Christians 'to speak evil of no one, to avoid quarrelling' in (Titus 3:2). Most of James 3 is about the tongue. What could be more damning than the language of Romans 3:13: 'their throat is an open grave'? This is a devouring, dark and ugly image. Every human heart can express this evil desire to entrap, ruin and destroy others. Indeed, the poison of vipers is 'under their lips.' One bite releases noxious poison into the intended victim. Cursing and bitterness fill the mouth. What person can say he has never done this, thought this, longed for this? From where does cursing God, others or circumstances come? These evils are the overflow of the heart. In Psalm 10, the passage behind Paul's words, the psalmist observes the treacherous use that people can make of others (Psa. 10:7–11).

Paul sums up this portion of Romans 3 by demonstrating that man's fallenness is shown by his actions (3:15–18):

'Their feet are swift to shed blood; in their paths are ruin and misery, and the way of peace they have not known.' If someone responds, 'I have not murdered, I have not shed blood,' the response is three-fold. First, which of us has not sinned in our hearts in these ways? This is the precise point made by our Lord Jesus in the Sermon on the Mount (cf. Matt. 5:21ff.) We have all murdered in our hearts, lusted in our hearts and retaliated in anger, at least internally. Second, this is the condition of the human race. The ways in which anger, hatred and bloodshed display the heart of man are legion. Third, outside of Christ, fallen man does nothing for God's glory. No act of fallen man is done for God's glory, not even those done from commitment to a moral philosophy. To say that no work outside of union with Christ is done for God's glory is to say that no work done outside of Christ is a good work. 'While you are not born again,' says Thomas Boston, 'your best works are but glittering sins.' He adds, 'Every corner [in the heart] is filled with that which of all things they have least liking for; and that is holiness, true holiness, perfect holiness.'[1]

The total inability of man
Scripture citations that show examples of man's depravity could be greatly multiplied. Furthermore, the depravity of man entails his total inability. Man is totally unable to do any good work, to save himself or to bring himself into a savable state.

---

[1] Boston, *Human Nature in Its Fourfold State*, pp. 243, 247.

Man's fall in Adam, his original sin and his actual sin, results in the inability of man to save himself, to regenerate himself or to contribute to his regeneration. This was a major theme of Jesus' discourse with Nicodemus. Nature cannot rise above nature. Men love darkness (John 3:19). Sinners refuse to come to Christ that they might have life (John 5:40). 'For the mind that is set on the flesh is hostile to God, for it does not submit to God's law; indeed, it cannot' (Rom. 8:7). Paul in 1 Corinthians 2:14 clearly teaches that the 'natural man,' the person outside of Christ, is incapable of saving himself: 'But the natural man receiveth not the things of the Spirit of God: for they are foolishness unto him: neither can he know them, because they are spiritually discerned' (AV). Jesus speaks of man's total inability in John 6:44: 'No one can come to me unless the Father who sent me draws him. And I will raise him up on the last day.' 'It is the Spirit who gives life; the flesh is no help at all' (6:63). 'No one can come to me unless it is granted him by the Father' (6:65). The reason why the natural man cannot perceive spiritual things and cannot come to Christ unaided is that 'The heart is deceitful above all things, and desperately wicked: who can know it?' (Jer. 17:9, AV). Paul declares in Romans 1 that sinners are truth-suppressors who deny God's clear self-revelation (Rom. 1:18ff.).

Satan also makes full use of man's innate depravity. Paul says, 'the god of this world has blinded the minds of the unbelievers, to keep them from seeing the light of the gospel of the glory of Christ, who is the image of God' (2 Cor. 4:4). Indeed, 'everyone who commits sin is a slave to sin' (John 8:34). Man's will is corrupt, in bondage and averse to God's law (Rom. 8:7). We are enemies to God in our minds (Col. 1:21).

> Set holiness and life upon the one side, sin and death upon the other; and leave the unrenewed will to itself, it will choose sin, and reject holiness. This is no more to be doubted, than that water poured on the side of a hill will run downward, and not upward; or that a flame will ascend and not descend.[1]

The Bible never flatters fallen human nature. Man's natural state is nothing less than dreadful. But is it hopeless? What is impossible for men is not impossible for God. The Heidelberg Catechism, 'Lord's Day' 3 in Q & A 8, supplies a biblical answer to the question of the sinner's hopelessness:

> Are we then so corrupt that we are wholly incapable of doing any good, and inclined to all wickedness? Indeed we are; except we are regenerated by the Spirit of God.

Hearing that the heart of the sinner is lost, undone, depraved, that none of us can bring ourselves to God and that, by nature, we do not want to return to God, that we are evil God-haters and can do no good thing certainly is not a popular message, but it is nonetheless true. Pointing to Romans 1:29, Thomas Boston says of original sin: 'There is a fullness of all unrighteousness there. … There is atheism, idolatry, blasphemy, murder, adultery, and whatever is vile.' These things are not apparent to blind sinners. But,

---

[1] Boston, *Human Nature in Its Fourfold State*, p. 102.

Boston says, the heart is like an ants' nest. When the stone covering the nest is removed and the ant bed stirred up, what a swarm is to be seen![1] This is what the Bible teaches about the human heart. The Westminster Confession (9.3) summarizes the issue powerfully:

> Man, by his fall into a state of sin, hath wholly lost all ability of will to any spiritual good accompanying salvation: so as, a natural man, being altogether averse from that good, and dead in sin, is not able by his own strength, to convert himself, or to prepare himself thereunto.

This is true of us all apart from regeneration. Oh, how infinitely great is our need!

If you are not yet born from above, I urge you to face these harsh realities. You need to trust in Christ, the only Redeemer of sinners. There is no hope apart from him. Every sinner who has departed from God is responsible for returning to the God from whom he has departed, even though incapable of doing so. Is there hope? Yes – but only by acknowledging your sin and finding refuge in Christ. There is hope in Christ and in no one and nowhere else.

---

[1] Boston, *Human Nature in Its Fourfold State*, p. 145.

7

How Sin Affects Our Minds and Wills

As a young, newly converted Christian, I regularly took my Bible and gospel tracts to the 'downtown' of my community and evangelized the lost. One of my encounters is indelibly printed on my mind. As I opened the gospel to a man sitting in front of a liquor store, he suddenly took out his false teeth covered with chewing tobacco and sincerely offered to sell them to me. 'I will sell them for a quarter,' he said. As a thirteen-year-old boy, raised in comfortable suburbs, and a new, inexperienced Christian, I was amazed. This needy man was so addicted to alcohol that he was willing to sell his teeth for the price of a shot of whisky! But as I continued to study my Bible about fallen human nature I came to understand that sin manifests itself in different ways but that all men, even 'moral' men, are just as bound in sin as that man with whom I spoke in front of the liquor store. As I have grown in grace over many years, I have realized many times over that my heart, apart from

Christ, has the same deep need as that man at the liquor store. Indeed, I think my need for salvation must be the greatest of them all.

We have looked at the necessity of regeneration by focusing on original sin, that is, the corruption of human nature due to the fall of Adam. We also noted that total depravity, the pervasive corruption of our entire nature, results in total inability. The sinner has no ability whatsoever to recover himself from his fallen estate. It is this point that needs stressing before we move on to look at regeneration itself. The biblical concept of regeneration will be radically altered if at any point we waver on this clear scriptural teaching.

Three passages on total inability

Of the many passages that teach total inability we will concentrate on three. We will look briefly at the teaching of Romans 1, 1 Corinthians 2:14 and Ephesians 4:17–18.

Romans 1

In Romans 1, Paul sets out the tragic consequences of the fall of man, seen largely in the Gentile world of his day. The first-century Gentile context, however, should not lead us to think that Paul's fundamental description is inapplicable to all sinners at all times. Remember, Paul, in the opening chapters of Romans, is showing that all sinners are incapable of life, that both Jews and Gentiles are under the wrath of God. In our previous chapter we briefly surveyed Romans 3 and noted that even though the actual sins of Gentiles and Jews may in some respects have differed, each human heart has the same fundamental need. In Romans 1, then, Paul shows the universal depravity and inability of sinners. How does he do this?

Paul does not indicate that sinners are simply damaged by the fall but are nonetheless capable of seeking the Lord. On the contrary, he must conclude of both Jew and Gentile that no sinner seeks God of his own volition. The entire world is guilty (3:19) and none seeks after God (3:11). As we saw in our two anchor texts, Jesus taught Nicodemus that sinners are 'flesh,' that is, morally corrupt, and Paul insists that sinners are dead in trespasses and sins (Eph. 2:1). Similarly, in Romans 1 Paul teaches that fallen sinners are truth-suppressors (1:18). As creatures of God, though fallen, everyone knows that God exists, his eternal power and Godhead being clearly manifested in every atom of the universe (1:18–21). No sooner do we sinners suppress one truth than up pops another, like a beach ball in a swimming pool. The sinner's entire life is one of suppressing what he knows to be true. In his antagonism against the God who is, every sinner's thinking has become foolish and darkened (verse 21). The problem is not with any lack of clarity in God's revelation of himself in nature; it is with man's reception of that revelation. Paul adds that, because sinners are exposed to the revelation of the divine perfections (verses 20–25, 32) and do not love, worship and serve God (verses 21, 25), they are inexcusable (1:20; 2:1) and, therefore, under God's wrath (1:18). Sinners exchange the truth of God for a lie (verses 23, 25, 28) and are even described by Paul as

God-haters (verse 30). One New Testament scholar put the matter profoundly when he said of the refrain 'God gave them over' (verses 24, 26, 28), 'the words sound to us like clods on the coffin as God leaves men to work their wicked will.'[1] In Romans 1, Paul describes the total depravity of man and his total inability to save himself.

1 Corinthians 2:14

In 1 Corinthians 2:14, Paul once again speaks plainly about the sinner's inability. In contrast to those who have received the things of God (2:11–13), the 'natural man receiveth not the things of the Spirit of God: for they are foolishness unto him: neither can he know them, because they are spiritually discerned' (2:14, AV). Clearly, the 'natural man' is contrasted with those who have the ability given them by the Holy Spirit to discern spiritual things. Those who have not received the Spirit of God (verses 11–12) are not able to search out and know the things of the Spirit. Here Paul clearly teaches that the sinner cannot receive and cannot know spiritual things. Paul's words describe *incapacity*, in two ways.

First, spiritual things are foolishness to the sinner. Therefore, he will not come to Christ. He has no desire to believe the gospel. He has no taste for it. Every converted sinner understands the meaning of this. Before conversion, the Bible and its contents were sealed and hidden; they made no sense and the heart was not attracted to them.

---

[1] A. T. Robertson, *Word Pictures in the New Testament* (Grand Rapids: Baker, reprint of 1931 original), vol. 4, p. 330.

But when the Spirit of God regenerates the sinner, he lives in a new world. Those things he once hated he now loves; those things that made no sense are suddenly his daily food and sustenance. The Bible in particular is a new book to those who have been born again. No sinner can work up this change; it is the result of regeneration.

Second, Paul speaks in bold terms of the sinner's incapacity to discern spiritual things. The sinner 'cannot' perceive them. Once again, it should be evident that because of original sin no sinner can change this in his own strength. He does not want to and he cannot will to. For this to change requires light to shine into the darkness of our lives, just as when God spoke in the original creation, 'Let there be light.' The indispensable element is the new creative work of God (2 Cor. 4:6; 5:17). Only those drawn by the Father will come to Christ (John 6:44). Sinners cannot know the things of God because they are spiritually discerned – that is, the regenerating and illuminating power of the Holy Spirit is indispensable. The infinitely wonderful Christ and his gospel are of no saving interest to those who are unregenerate. The sinner's depravity is his natural habitat, shaping all that he does.

Ephesians 4:17–18
In this context Paul describes the new walk of the believer in Christ. But Paul finds it necessary to remind his readers of what they were before they came to know Christ. He first mentions 'the futility of their minds [or thinking].' The word 'futility' carries with it the notion of aimlessness.

The goal of God's glory is completely missed (Rom. 3:23) since there is 'no fear of God before their eyes' (Rom. 3:18).

But the problem with the unbeliever is not simply one of inadequate information. Paul says that unbelievers are 'darkened in their understanding.' The abundantly clear revelation of God stares the unbeliever in the face and is, in fact, part of his own being. Yet sinners are darkened until the Holy Spirit creates in them a clean heart and enlightens their mind. Sinners, thus, were 'alienated from the life of God.' Sinners have no fellowship with God. 'Your iniquities have made a separation between you and your God' (Isa. 59:2). Sinners who do not believe the gospel will be permanently alienated from God. This alienation is due to 'the ignorance that is in them.' That ignorance is not lack of education, but sinful ignorance. Sinful ignorance cannot see the light of the gospel unaided. The moral darkness of the lost soul is worse than a million midnights in a Florida swamp. Indeed, their ignorance is due to their 'hardness of heart.' This manifests itself in lust for impurity. Out-of-control, insatiable appetites are meant here. Sinful man loves his sin; he craves his own way. He would rather have his sin than salvation. He would rather be damned for eternity than part with his sinful lusts. Verse 22 uses the verb 'corrupt' in the present tense to indicate that the sinner's heart can grow more and more corrupt.

Thankfully, Paul does not stop there! He goes on to show how the moral image of God lost in the fall is restored in Christ. However, this passage is one of many that underscores the total corruption and inability of sinners to save themselves. The mind and affections are corrupt, sinners are not able to discern spiritual things and the whole soul is in spiritual death (Eph. 2:1). By nature, sinners are under the power of darkness (Col. 1:13), are enemies of God (Col. 1:21) and have perverse wills (Eph. 2:3); therefore, no sinner can regenerate himself. That is the great conclusion to be drawn from these and similar texts of Scripture.

An ancient but very modern heresy

The primary distinction between a biblical and an unbiblical concept of regeneration is at just this point: the Bible pervasively teaches that no sinner can bring himself to regeneration and conversion. Though responsible to believe and repent, he is unable to do so. At this point we are compelled to remember the ancient heresy of Pelagianism and to bemoan the ongoing influence of this grace-denying teaching in the life of the church.

Perhaps today more than ever the Pelagian heresy and its variant, semi-Pelagianism, thrive. In the early fifth century Pelagius opposed the emphasis of Augustine (one of the great early church leaders) on grace. Pelagius essentially denied original sin, insisting that people do not sin because they are sinners, but that they learn sin and transgress according to their own self-determination. If that were not so, he maintained, there could be no human responsibility. Contrary to the Bible's teaching about the disposition of sinners fallen in Adam, Pelagianism and its various expressions hold that man's nature is not bad, or at least, it is not as bad as the Bible says it is. Particularly in the form of Pelagianism taught by the seventeenth century Dutch theologian James Arminius and his followers, the will is viewed as having the ability to choose or reject salvation, perhaps with some aid from God. God cannot, according to this view, intervene in a sinner's life in the sovereignty of his will and grace. In the Arminian perspective, the one thing that must be maintained is the sovereignty of the will of man. How contrary all of this is to the Bible's teaching of the fall of man, original sin, the sinner's bondage in mind and will to iniquity and the condition of the sinner as dead in trespasses and sins! As Matthew 7:18 says, 'A healthy tree cannot bear bad fruit, *nor can a diseased tree bear good fruit.*' All of us, by nature, are diseased trees unable to bear good fruit. We need regeneration.

Regeneration is not just moral persuasion

The Bible's teaching means that the popular notion that regeneration is simply moral persuasion cannot be even near the truth. This is seen especially in the influence of Charles G. Finney, a nineteenth-century popular lawyer-turned-preacher who taught that by simply using means to persuade, sinners could choose the new birth. When one evangelistic approach did not work any longer, the approach needed to be altered to find another that would. This is not biblical and is not the approach of the sound evangelism of notable evangelists in the history of the church such as George Whitefield or Jonathan Edwards, both of whom saw many people brought to faith in Christ during the eighteenth-century revival in Britain and

America. Finney's view, though immensely popular and influential, is the polar opposite of historic, evangelical Christianity.

Yes, when the gospel is presented to sinners, we address that gospel to men and women who have minds and wills. Argument and persuasion are necessary for the proper presentation of the gospel. We ask sinners, 'Why will you perish?' We give reasons why they should come to Christ. We remind people that the Bible calls them to faith and repentance. However, the true preacher of the gospel knows that only as the Spirit of God accompanies this kind of preaching with regenerating and converting power will sinners respond. We preach, as it were, in a cemetery, but with the knowledge that God can give life to the dead (Eph. 2:4, 5).

John Owen's observations [1]

John Owen is regarded by many as one of the most influential theologians of the seventeenth-century Puritan era and, indeed, of all time. In his magnificent book on the Holy Spirit he makes three essential observations about the erroneous view that regeneration is according to man's will and is the mere result of moral persuasion.

First, if that is so, then the whole glory of regeneration must be ascribed to ourselves and not to God. It is evident that if we effectively regenerate ourselves, the glory goes to man and not to God for the salvation of the soul. But, as

---

[1] For what follows, see John Owen, *Discourse on the Holy Spirit* in *Works of John Owen* (Edinburgh: Banner of Truth Trust, 1981), vol. 3, pp. 308–312.

Owen observes, 'If the act itself were of grace, then would it not be in the power of the will to hinder it.' Grace, if it be grace, must be effectual.

Second, Owen observed that the Arminian viewpoint on regeneration being attained by moral persuasion would leave uncertain whether anyone would ever be converted. 'For then,' says Owen, 'the whole work of grace is over, it is absolutely in the power of the will of man whether it shall be effectual or no, and so absolutely uncertain: which is contrary to the covenant, promise, and oath of God unto and with Jesus Christ.' If left to man, regeneration would be uncertain; indeed, in view of what Scripture teaches, it would not happen at all. Then all that Scripture teaches about God, his sovereign will and his grace and salvation are taken as nothing.

Third, Owen observes that the Arminian concept that man by an act of the will can choose to be regenerated is contrary to innumerable scripture passages in which we find conversion to God ascribed to the immediacy of grace. For example, Philippians 2:13 says, 'For it is God who works in you, both to will and to work for his good pleasure.' Think also of Lydia, whose heart the Lord opened to heed Paul's preaching (Acts 16:14). Indeed, behind every conversion is the electing purpose of God. As many as are appointed to eternal life will believe (Acts 13:48).

Owen continues to argue that, if human ability and not God's free grace is the basis, then prayer for the unregenerate would be a farce. To summarize: we would be mocking God, asking him to do what we can do for ourselves and that which it is claimed God cannot do because, it is thought, if God sovereignly regenerates, he does violence to the will of man. This leads to the commonplace but important observation that every Christian is a Calvinist on his knees.

Having closely examined the Bible's teaching about our lost condition, we turn next in more depth to the sovereign regeneration without which we cannot enter God's kingdom.

8

Born of God

Every sinner's need is desperate. Their minds are at enmity with God (Gen. 3:15; Rom. 8:7; Col. 1:21). Man, since the fall, no longer bears the image of God in knowledge, righteousness and holiness (Col. 3:10; Eph. 4:23–24). Every sinner is a suppressor of truth (Rom. 1:18). Nineteenth-century American pastor George Bethune wrote in his work on the Heidelberg Catechism:

> When the will is exercised, there is choice; and when we say that man cannot, before he is regenerate, choose the service of God, we do not mean that he is compelled to evil by a force without himself, as a stream runs downward or a flame points upward; but that he is so wicked by nature that his choice is inevitably fixed on what is wrong. He cannot do right, because he is so bent on doing wrong. Can any of us say that he is forced to sin whether he will or not? Can he say that his bondage to sin does not include his will, or that, when he sins, he is not a voluntary agent? There is no reasoning on this; we know it, in the same way that we know we exist, from our consciousness. If, then, we sin of

our own accord, can we be innocent? Nay, if we are without a disposition to obey God, there can be no doubt of our guilt. It is the want of a heart to serve him for which God condemns us. The inability spoken of by the word of God and the Catechism, is nothing else than the depravity of our nature through sin by which our heart is alienated from God, our understanding blinded, and our very conscience perverted. Therefore (in the language of the Episcopal Church), 'the condition of man after the fall, is such, that he cannot turn and prepare himself, by his own natural strength and good works, unto faith and calling of God.'[1]

In himself, the sinner is hopeless. But God can do what man cannot.

Bill sat in the back rows of our church for a year hearing the gospel. Every Sunday he quickly left after the benediction. He was an esteemed physician who had never attended church services previously. Science, at least his idea of science, he later confessed, was his god. But one day, Bill walked into my study. 'Pastor,' he said, 'I don't know what's happened to me. I didn't believe, and now I do.' Bill was born again. Everything had changed for him. He now wanted to study God's word. He applied his new-found faith to his home, medical practice and personal life. He has now been a faithful follower of Christ for many years. God can do what man cannot.

A young woman came to me after a service and her words were almost precisely the same as Bill's: 'Pastor, I just

---

[1] George W. Bethune, *Guilt, Grace and Gratitude: Lectures on the Heidelberg Catechism* (Edinburgh: Banner of Truth Trust, 2001), vol. 1, p. 81.

don't understand. I didn't want to worship, but now I long to worship and hear the word.' This young lady was born again. For years now the fruit of the new birth has been clearly evident in her life. God can do what man cannot.

The Heidelberg Catechism, a catechism that has confessional status in many churches of Reformation heritage, excellently summarizes the Bible's teaching on sin, depravity and the necessity of the new birth in the section Lord's Day 3. In the prior section, following the words 'I am prone by nature to hate God and my neighbour,' the Catechism continues:

> Q. 6. Did God then make man so wicked and perverse?
> A. By no means; but God created man good, and after his own image, in true righteousness and holiness, that he might rightly know God his Creator, heartily love him and live with him in eternal happiness to glorify and praise him.

> Q. 7. Whence then proceeds this depravity of human nature?
> A. From the fall and disobedience of our first parents, Adam and Eve, in Paradise; hence our nature is become so corrupt, that we are all conceived and born in sin.

> Q. 8. Are we so corrupt that we are wholly incapable of doing any good, and inclined to all wickedness?
> A. Indeed we are; except we are regenerated by the Spirit of God.

'Except we are regenerated by the Spirit of God,' says the Catechism, and that is precisely what God does in the lives of his elect.

The Arminian model

You will remember that one of the anchor texts with which we began to look into the Bible's teaching on regeneration was the conversation between Jesus and Nicodemus in John 3. In that conversation, the Lord Jesus instructed Nicodemus that nature cannot rise above nature. The Scriptures constantly lead us to the conclusion that man's mind, will and affections are not simply impaired by the fall of the human race in Adam, but are ruined. Despite this clear scriptural teaching, many Christian circles set up unbiblical models of regeneration. We have already mentioned two false but intimately related models regarding regeneration largely based upon a faulty view of man's fallen condition: Pelagianism and its Arminian manifestation. Although it is not obvious on the surface, this view is deeply embedded in the understanding of salvation preached by many churches.

In its popular form, the Pelagian viewpoint goes something like this: 'Yes, we may speak of sin in some way, but after all, we must insist that man is basically good and it is within every person's ability to straighten his life out morally and to reform his attitudes.' For example, my wife Vicky once gave a recording of one of my sermons to a neighbour. After a few days, Vicky questioned her about the sermon. Our neighbour said, 'The sermon was good, except when he spoke of sin. You see, I am an educator. I believe that what we call sin is a problem of lack of education. As education improves, "sin" goes away.' This friend probably did not know the term 'Pelagian' but the position she expressed was the Pelagian one. The idea is that man is a blank slate. There is no original sin. People learn bad things along the way, but that can be overcome by natural means. This woman had never seen the depth of her need before the holy God. It may well be true that sinners can reform themselves in many ways – but self-reformation is not regeneration.

In evangelical churches, however, the most prevalent view of regeneration is what is often labelled 'semi-Pelagian,' that is, the Arminian viewpoint. This is vigorously preached in many evangelical circles. The Arminian approach claims that even though man is fallen, his will is relatively unaffected. Therefore, regeneration is in the hands of the sinner. In my youth I heard it put this way: 'On the matter of the new birth, God casts a vote, the devil casts a vote but you cast the deciding vote.' There are two problems with such a view. First, it dishonours God's attributes and sovereignty. God is represented as one whose hands are tied, unable to apply salvation to the sinner unless and until the sinner permits it. Second, it ignores the biblical teaching about the depravity of man.

Arminianism tries to maintain human responsibility but does so by stressing human autonomy. In its most popular forms, it maintains that God cannot require of sinners that which they themselves are not capable of doing. But the Scriptures teach otherwise. Fallen in Adam, the whole human race is responsible to return to the God from whom we have departed, even though we are incapable of doing this on our own. Additionally, Arminianism does not see that responsibility cannot be maintained against the backdrop of chance. As the Westminster Confession so beautifully teaches, second causes can only have meaning in a universe in which God rules.[1]

The eighteenth-century preacher and evangelist John Wesley argued with regard to human responsibility, 'Men are free in believing or not believing,' and 'if man were not free, he could not be accountable either for his thoughts, words, or actions.'[2] But this view contradicts the plain teaching of Scripture and confuses things that differ. Ability and responsibility are not equivalent to each other.

The Holy Spirit: the only one who can bring about regeneration

We have seen how the Scriptures teach that man is not merely damaged by the fall, not simply impaired, but lost and ruined. It is not scriptural to view regeneration as mere persuasion brought about by a minister or evangelist, or as the Spirit simply applying a little pressure, so ultimately the sinner makes the decision to be regenerated. Regeneration is not cooperation between God and the sinner. From first to last, regeneration is a result of God's sovereign freedom, the wind blowing where it wills, the choice of God the

---

[1] Confession of Faith, 3.1: 'God from all eternity, did, by the most wise and holy counsel of His own will, freely, and unchangeably ordain whatsoever comes to pass: yet so as thereby neither is God the author of sin, nor is violence offered to the will of the creatures; nor is the liberty or contingency of second causes taken away, but rather established.'

[2] John Wesley, *Sermons on Several Occasions* (London: John Mason, 1863), vol. 2, p. 227.

Father, the salvation purchased by the Son applied to the chosen and purchased sinner by the almighty Spirit of God. How can a sinner, dead in trespasses and sins, bring himself to life, spark the beginning of grace in his soul or cooperate at will to raise himself from spiritual death? Would that not give to the sinner something to boast about (Eph. 2:9)? 'For who sees anything different in you? What do you have that you did not receive? If then you received it, why do you boast as if you did not receive it?' (1 Cor. 4:7). Rather than confessing with the Scriptures that 'God chose what is low and despised in the world, even things that are not, to bring to nothing things that are, so that no human being might boast in the presence of God,' would the sinner not, after all, have something about which to glory?

The Bible teaches that God is the source of our life in Christ Jesus, whom God made our 'wisdom ... righteousness and sanctification and redemption'; therefore, 'let the one who boasts, boast in the Lord' (1 Cor 1:30, 31). Given the Arminian viewpoint, however, the sinner might indeed boast: 'I am, after all, the source of my life in Christ.' No theory of salvation dishonours God more greatly in this matter than the Arminian one which declares man's will to be sovereign over God's. 'Not to us, O Lord, not to us, but to your name give glory' (Psa. 115:1) must ever be the song of praise streaming from the hearts of regenerate people.

A lost sinner, dead in sin, can neither save himself nor bring himself into a savable state. By nature we are helpless, without strength, ungodly and enemies of God (Rom. 5:6–8). The life of the Holy Spirit must be breathed into a sinner's soul that he might become alive and believe on Christ. 'But to all who did receive him, who believed in his name, he gave the right to become children of God, who were born, not of blood nor of the will of the flesh nor of the will of man, but of God' (John 1:12, 13). God's saving mercy 'depends not on human will or exertion, but on God, who has mercy' (Rom. 9:16). Without the new birth, sinners cannot see the kingdom of God (John 3:3). Without the new birth, sinners remain 'flesh,' rebellious creatures opposed to God (John 3:6), and are lost, undone and insensible to divine things until the Holy Spirit grants regeneration. 'The wind blows where it wishes, and you hear its sound, but you do not know where it comes from or where it goes. So it is with everyone who is born of the Spirit' (John 3:8).

The Scriptures are clear: man is not born again of his own will but of the will and in the power of God. The new birth is not a cooperative effort between God and the sinner. The sinner must believe in Christ for justification, but from where does this faith come to those who, by nature, are dead in trespasses and sins? The Heidelberg Catechism superbly summarizes biblical teaching in question and answer 65:

> Q. Since then we are made partakers of Christ and all his benefits by faith only, whence does this faith proceed?
>
> A. From the Holy Ghost, who works faith in our hearts by the preaching of the gospel, and confirms it by the use of the sacraments.

The Catechism accurately summarizes the teaching of God's word: the source of faith is the Holy Spirit. It is the Holy Spirit 'who works faith in our hearts.' In his natural state the sinner, dead in sin, cannot enter God's kingdom. He may hear the gospel with the natural ear, but he cannot believe the gospel apart from Spirit-produced faith: 'The natural person does not accept the things of the Spirit of God, for they are folly to him, and he is not able to understand them because they are spiritually discerned' (1 Cor. 2:14). It is the Spirit of God alone who can enable sinners to believe the gospel. The sinner must be renewed within in order to embrace Jesus Christ freely offered in the gospel. The Holy Spirit does not believe for us; we must believe. However, we can only believe when that faith is Holy Spirit-wrought.

This faith is brought about in the hearts of believers in harmony with man's rational nature. The Holy Spirit does not cause us to act against our wills; rather, he sweetly and effectually changes our wills so that we freely embrace Christ and believe his gospel. The Holy Spirit convinces us of sin (John 16:8) and blesses the preaching of his word as the gospel minister 'persuades' sinners to believe and repent (2 Cor. 5:11). The same Holy Spirit who was at work in the raising of Jesus from the dead must operate in dead sinners to bring them to life (Eph. 1:19, 20), thus 'enlightening' our hearts (Eph. 1:18). This is how the Holy Spirit mysteriously and powerfully enables sinners to be saved, to see and to enter the kingdom of God. Apart from this Spirit-wrought life, faith in Christ would be impossible.

God at work

Thus, in the biblical understanding of regeneration, there is no cooperative effort between God and man. Regeneration is God's work quite apart from any contribution of man; it is God who sovereignly raises dead sinners to life. This is evident in the two key texts of John 3 and Ephesians 2. The Holy Spirit acts according to his own will in regeneration, as Jesus taught Nicodemus in John 3. Moreover, dead sinners are raised to life by God's power, according to Ephesians 2. This is the consistent teaching of the Bible. The only efficient means of regeneration is the Holy Spirit. Man cannot bring about his own conversion.

As with Lydia, Paul's first convert in Philippi, our sinful hearts must be opened (Acts 16:14). We must be given a heart of flesh (Ezek. 36:26), our eyes must be enlightened (Eph. 1:18), there needs to be new birth (John 3; James 1:18), a new heart must be created (Psa. 51:10) and the resurrection life of Jesus must raise the spiritually dead to life (Eph. 1:19; 2:1, 4–6).

If we keep the biblical portrait of our fallen condition to the fore, this will be an effective antidote to the idea that our cooperation with God through 'free will' brings about our own regeneration. New birth takes us from death to life. It requires the all-commanding voice of God to call us to new life just as really as the body of Lazarus required our Saviour's 'Come forth' to bring him back to life. We are not regenerated by self-determined free agency, but by the almighty power of the sovereign God of free grace.

The place of God's word

We next need to ask whether or not God uses means to bring about the new birth. That is, given that sinners are dead in trespasses and sins and are incapable of saving themselves, God must impart the life for them not only to hear, but also to understand and respond to the gospel. However, James 1:18 and 1 Peter 1:23 seem to suggest that God also uses means to bring this about. We see this especially in 1 Peter 1:23, which speaks of our being born again 'through the living and abiding word of God.'

It may be helpful to realize that the term 'regeneration' is sometimes used in a narrower and sometimes in a broader sense. The sixteenth-century Reformers tended to speak not just of the Spirit's initial granting of life but also of everything involved in conversion as regeneration. Later Reformed theology, however, tended to narrow the term to the moment the Holy Spirit imparts life to the spiritually dead.

The Scriptures too, however, seem to use 'new birth' in both the narrower and the broader senses. John 3 and Ephesians 2 stress the initial life-giving power of the Holy Spirit. More broadly, 1 Peter 1:23 and James 1:18 seem to stress not only the initial life-giving power of the Spirit, but also the Spirit's use of God's word. Of course, the language of 1 Peter 1:23 cannot be taken to mean that the word works apart from the Holy Spirit. How do we relate the immediacy of the Spirit's work and the Spirit's use of his word in regeneration?

First, there is the coming together of the Spirit's regenerating work and the proclamation of the word in preaching. The ordinary way that God brings people to new life in Christ is in the context of the preaching of the word (though not when it comes to how God works salvation in infants). When the Holy Spirit sovereignly gives life from the dead, it is to enable saving faith to embrace Jesus Christ in the proclamation of the gospel. One Anglican clergyman of the past, Bishop Hopkins, said it well: 'when God new creates man, he breathes into his ears.'[1] Just as God breathed the breath of life into Adam, so the Lord grants a new ability to receive the truth. Another commentator, Robert Leighton, writes about 1 Peter 1:23,

> The preacher of the word, be he never so powerful, can cast this seed only into the ear; his hand reaches no farther; and the hearer, by his attention, may convey it to his head; but it is the supreme Father and Teacher above, who carries it into the heart, the only soil wherein it proves lively and fruitful.

He adds: 'But though this word cannot beget without Him, yet it is by this word that He begets, and ordinarily not without it.'[2]

Second, since the word does not possess inherent power to regenerate but must be accompanied by the immediate and effective power of God's Spirit, clearly, regeneration (in the narrow sense) is immediate. However, the Spirit

[1] Cited by J. C. Ryle, *Knots Untied* (Edinburgh: Banner of Truth Trust, 2016), p. 127.

[2] Robert Leighton, *Commentary on 1 Peter* (Grand Rapids: Kregel, 1978), pp. 105, 106.

ordinarily uses his word as the means to bring this about. The Spirit and his inspired word do not stand opposed! Calvin's words apply here:

> For the Lord has so knit together the certainty of his word and his Spirit, that our minds are duly imbued with reverence for the word when the Spirit shining upon it enables us there to behold the face of God; and, on the other hand, we embrace the Spirit with no danger of delusion when we recognize him in his image, that is, in his word.[1]

Theologians of an older generation correctly distinguished between the Holy Spirit as the efficient cause of regeneration and the word used by the Spirit as the instrumental cause. Along these lines, and in line with the Reformed theologians of the past, Sinclair Ferguson astutely observed,

> Since the Spirit's work in regeneration involves the transformation of the whole man, including his cognitive and affective powers, the accompanying of the internal illumination of the Spirit by the external revelation of the word (and vice versa) is altogether appropriate. Since faith involves knowledge, it ordinarily emerges in relationship to the teaching of the gospel found in Scripture. Regeneration and the faith to which it gives birth are seen as taking place not by revelationless divine sovereignty, but within the matrix of the preaching of the word and the witness of the people of God (cf. Rom. 10:1–15). Their instrumentality in

---

[1] John Calvin, *Institutes of the Christian Religion*, trans. Henry Beveridge (Grand Rapids: Eerdmans, 1964), I.ix.3, p. 86.

regeneration does not impinge upon the sovereign activity of the Spirit. Word and Spirit belong together.[1]

Seen in light of Jesus' parable of the soils (Matt. 13:1–23), the good seed (God's word) must fall on good soil in order to take root. 'Good soil' is the one who has been given new life from God. The gospel is the power of God unto salvation to those who believe (Rom. 1:16), but faith embracing the gospel is the result of the Spirit's regenerating work in a person's life. Herman Bavinck, a Dutch theologian whose work spanned the end of the nineteenth and the early twentieth centuries, observed that regeneration occurs under, by and with the word, but not through the word 'in the sense that the Holy Spirit could work with the human heart only through the Word.' He notes that the Holy Spirit

> has indeed bound Himself to creating fellowship with Christ and His benefits where the Word of Christ is proclaimed; but He has neither imprisoned nor enclosed Himself and His operation within the Word.[2]

We should consider this work of God in the soul with awe. Regeneration is, in the superb language of the Canons of Dordt (3.4.12),

> a supernatural work, most powerful, and at the same time most delightful, astonishing, mysterious, and ineffable; not inferior in efficacy to creation or the resurrection from

[1] Sinclair B. Ferguson, *The Holy Spirit* (Downers Grove, IL.: InterVarsity Press, 1996), pp. 125, 126.

[2] Herman Bavinck, *Saved By Grace: The Holy Spirit's Work in Calling and Regeneration* (Grand Rapids: Reformation Heritage, 2008), p. 152.

the dead, as the Scripture inspired by the author of this work declares; so that all in whose heart God works in this marvellous manner are certainly, infallibly, and effectually regenerated, and do actually believe. Whereupon the will thus renewed is not only actuated and influenced by God, but in consequence of this influence, becomes itself active. Wherefore also, man is himself rightly said to believe and repent, by virtue of that grace received.

The use of the preached word by the Holy Spirit is neither contradiction nor threat to divine sovereignty. Instead of denigrating the word, Reformed evangelism has the primacy of preaching as its hallmark. For example, suppose I go outside and you see me from your window cutting down an oak tree with a chain saw. You might think little of it. But suppose you observe me take out my pocket knife and cut down the tree with that. You would be amazed! 'What power!' you would exclaim. So it is when the minister, in and of himself an ineffective instrument, preaches the word of God; thought by men to be foolish, in the hand of the Holy Spirit it is like the pocket knife that fells the mighty oak! R. L. Dabney, a nineteenth-century pastor-theologian of the Southern Presbyterian Church in America, beautifully summarized the relationship between the Holy Spirit and the word proclaimed in regeneration: 'The Holy Ghost renovates the mental vision; the word of God alone furnishes the luminous medium through which the renovated vision sees.'[1]

---

[1] R. L. Dabney, *Systematic Theology* (Edinburgh: Banner of Truth Trust, 1985), pp. 564; 560. The above illustration is based on Dabney's.

The idea of baptismal regeneration

It might be helpful to think briefly about the link between baptism and regeneration. Some churches, most obviously the Roman Catholic Church as well as many others of Anglo-Catholic persuasion, believe that regeneration is the internal effect of baptism and that all who are baptized receive the new birth conveying the forgiveness of sins and the removal of guilt. This new birth, however, does not always develop into spiritual life.[1] This view is based, in part, on the mistaken notion that the 'water' in John 3:5, 'unless one is born of water and the Spirit, he cannot enter the kingdom of God,' refers to Christian baptism. Christian baptism, however, had not yet been instituted at that point and the reference would have been meaningless to Nicodemus. It is more likely that 'water' simply refers to the Spirit's cleansing. The 'and' is explanatory; as Calvin says, 'by *water* is meant nothing more than the inward purification and invigoration which is produced by *the Holy Spirit.*'[2] The baptismal regeneration viewpoint also fails to understand the concept of 'sacramental union.' This may be a difficult concept but it needs to be understood. 'Sacramental union' means that the grace signified is metaphorically attributed to the sign itself. So, when Peter preaches 'Repent and be baptized … for the forgiveness of your sins' (Acts 2:38), he no more intends for his hearers to understand that baptism

---

[1] See, for example, Claude Beaufort Moss, *The Christian Faith: An Introduction to Dogmatic Theology* (London: SPCK, 1954), pp. 341ff.

[2] John Calvin, *Commentary on the Gospel according to John* in *Calvin's Commentaries* (Grand Rapids: Baker, 1979), vol. 17, p. 111.

actually produces forgiveness of sins than David intended his readers to understand hyssop as effecting spiritual cleansing when he prayed, 'Purge me with hyssop, and I shall be clean' (Psa. 51:7). While baptism is not a bare sign, it does not bring about regeneration in the person baptized. As nineteenth-century American theologian A. A. Hodge observed, 'There is nothing said of the efficacy of Baptism which is not likewise said of the efficacy of truth … but the mere hearing of truth saves no one.'[1]

Trust nothing and no one but Christ

The idea of baptismal regeneration is dangerous because it can direct one's attention from what is signified (salvation through Christ) to the sign itself, leading a sinner to trust in the outward act of baptism rather than in Christ. We need to hear this warning: do not trust anything or anyone but Christ for salvation from sin. Do not trust church membership, family connections or futile attempts at finding righteousness through good works; nothing and no one can save but Christ alone.

God gives the new birth, but I am still responsible?

'But wait,' says someone who is not a believer in Christ, 'you have been stressing in this chapter that sinners can only be regenerated if the Holy Spirit performs this work. Yet you tell me to trust in Christ.' Yes, the sinner is responsible to return to the God from whom he has departed even though

---

[1] A. A. Hodge, *The Confession of Faith* (Edinburgh: Banner of Truth Trust, 1983), p. 350.

he is incapable of doing so apart from the new birth. However, very often when the Spirit of God regenerates, this very fact of our inability is used to bring us to the point at which we cast ourselves on Christ alone for salvation.

The nineteenth-century Presbyterian pastor-theologian B. M. Palmer tells of such an experience in his first ministry.[1] Palmer had been faithfully preaching that sinners cannot save themselves while, simultaneously, calling sinners to trust in Christ. A young guest who had attended services became very perturbed by this preaching and one day barged in on Palmer in his study. 'You preachers are the most contradictory men in the world; you say, and you unsay, just as it pleases you,' said the young man, 'without the least pretence of consistency.' Palmer was not surprised at the outburst, and he calmly asked the youth to elaborate. The young man said: 'Why, yesterday you said in your sermon that sinners were perfectly helpless in themselves—utterly unable to repent and believe, and then turned square round and said that they would all be damned if they did not.' Palmer replied: 'Well … there is no use in our quarrelling over this matter; either you can or you cannot. If you can, all I have to say is that I hope you will just go and do it.' Palmer had not taken his eyes off his writing desk the entire time, but after a moment heard the choking reply: 'I have been trying my best for three whole days, and cannot.' The wise pastor put down

---

[1] Thomas Cary Johnson, *The Life and Letters of Benjamin Morgan Palmer* (Edinburgh: Banner of Truth Trust, 1987), pp. 83, 84.

his pen and replied: 'Ah, that puts a different face upon it; we will go then and tell the difficulty straight out to God.' The pastor and young man knelt together and the pastor pleaded for divine intervention. He left the young man 'in his powerlessness in the hands of God, as the only helper.' Shortly thereafter his struggles were over and the young man came to conscious faith in Christ. Is it you who now needs to go down on his knees and cry out to the only Helper for salvation?

9

Understanding God's Order of Salvation

I n all important things in life it is essential to think in the right order. A cook needs to follow the right order of a recipe. An electrician must be careful to do certain things in order so that the job is done correctly and safely. A preacher must understand the text and present it with logical order so that his sermon is heard and is effective. The Scriptures also give to us a right order for understanding the plan of salvation. Theologians refer to this using the Latin term *ordo salutis*—'order of salvation.'

We derive our understanding of this order from the divinely inspired source, Holy Scripture. *Ordo salutis* is a mental map that helps us understand how the different components of salvation fit together, especially with regard to regeneration and faith. If we fail to understand the place of the new birth in this mapping exercise, we will diminish God's glory in our thinking on this matter, with disastrous results for gospel preaching and personal piety.

Is a mental map necessary?

The concept of *ordo salutis* is too often dismissed today. Yet, if we get back to teaching tools used by former generations of Christians, we may be forced to think again. William Perkins, the 'father of English Puritanism,' developed from the Scriptures a Christ-centred map of how the plan of salvation should be viewed, called 'the golden chain.' He understood that even though the Bible relates the history of salvation – planned in eternity, revealed through promise, precept and prophecy in the Old Testament, accomplished with the coming of Christ, explained by the apostles and finally brought to consummation when Jesus returns – it is still necessary to understand the component parts of salvation.

Throughout church history there has been a long and respected tradition of exploring the individual parts of how God's truth 'fits together.' When this is done in faithfulness to God's word we find that the component parts of salvation are held together by the person and work of Jesus Christ.

Union with Christ

Understanding the right order of salvation begins with understanding what it means for the Christian to be united to Christ by faith. If you happen to be a new Christian, please tuck away in your mind my counsel to read Calvin's *Institutes of the Christian Religion* at some point early in your Christian life, and to return to it many times. It may be a challenge, but there is little that can help you to understand God's word as much as this hugely important work. On this matter of 'mental map,' Calvin asks, how do we receive the benefits of Christ? With keen biblical insight he answers that

> as long as Christ remains outside of us, and we are separated from him, all that he has suffered and done for the salvation of the human race remains useless and of no value to us.[1]

Thus, Calvin, in line with Paul, puts our union with Christ at the centre of our thinking about how redemption is applied to us personally. In another place, Calvin argues that

> our whole salvation and all its parts are comprehended in Christ. We should therefore take care not to derive the least portion of it from anywhere else.[2]

In these statements Calvin is simply saying what we find constantly in the writings of the apostle Paul in particular, namely, that all of our blessings are found in Christ alone (Eph. 1:3). All spiritual blessings are found in union with Christ.

Union with Christ is a multi-faceted truth and its components are far reaching. They involve the following:[3]

• *A comprehensive union.* It is not simply a stage in our

---

[1] John Calvin, *Institutes of the Christian Religion* (Philadelphia: Westminster Press, 1960), III.i.1.

[2] Calvin, *Institutes*, II.xvi.19. This section is a must-read and one of the most deeply devotional passages in all theology.

[3] Compare A. A. Hodge, *Outlines of Theology* (Grand Rapids: Zondervan, 1980), pp. 483–484. Also see Sinclair B. Ferguson, *Know Your Christian Life* (Downers Grove, IL: InterVarsity Press, 1981), pp. 92–101.

salvation but comprehensive of all of salvation, the hub from which all of the spokes stem. We are chosen in Christ, we died in union with Christ's death, we were buried in his burial, we were raised in his resurrection, we will be in him when we die (body and soul) and we will be in union with Christ for ever – nothing will separate us from the love of God in Christ.

• *A representative union.* The entire human race is either in Adam or in Christ. If you are in Adam, you are lost; if in Christ, you are saved.

• *A spiritual union.* Union with Christ is actuated and sustained by the Holy Spirit.

• *A faith union.* We become actual partakers of Christ and of all his benefits by faith.

• *A life-giving union.* Just as the branches receive life-giving sap from the roots and trunk of the tree, so we are given life by union with Christ. We are raised 'in Christ' to walk in newness of life.

• *A union of communion.* By union with Christ we have fellowship with the triune God.

• *A fraternal union.* We are bound to one another as believers because of our union with Christ (Rom. 12:5).

• *A mysterious union.* Paul derives his understanding of marriage in Ephesians 5 from our union with Christ. If we cannot define the mysterious union between a husband and wife, we certainly cannot exhaust the mystery of our union with Christ.

• *An eternal union.* Since it is grounded in God's eternal decree and the actual accomplishment of redemption, those in union with Christ are in union for eternity and nothing can sever that union! Our union with Christ is indissoluble!

While space will not allow us to unpack in depth what union with Christ means, the point is to see clearly that, as Calvin said, we possess no benefit from Christ as long as Christ remains outside of us. As we have mentioned already, union with Christ is comprehensive. We are chosen in Christ (Eph. 1:4). We died in union with Christ's death (Rom. 6:3) and were buried in his burial (Rom. 6:4). We also were raised in Christ's resurrection (Rom. 6:4) and ascended in him (Eph. 2:4–6). When the believer dies, his body and soul are united to Christ (1 Thess. 4:16) and shall be in union with Christ for ever (Rom 8:28-39). Twentieth-century Scottish theologian John Murray beautifully summarized the matter when he wrote:

> The perspective of God's people is not narrow; it is broad and it is long. It is not confined to space and time; it has the expanse of eternity. Its orbit has two foci, one the electing love of God the Father in the counsels of eternity, the other glorification with Christ in the manifestation of his glory. The former has no beginning, the latter has no end.[1]

We need to go on to explore the connection between union with Christ and regeneration, and why it is important to keep this map in mind in how we think about salvation.

---

[1] John Murray, *Redemption Accomplished and Applied* (Edinburgh: Banner of Truth Trust, 2016), p. 168.

Union with Christ and regeneration

The Christian's personal union with Christ is brought about by the regenerating work of the Holy Spirit. Regeneration is, on the one hand, *a benefit of* our union with Christ – that is, it is a result of our election in union with Christ before the foundation of the world (Eph. 1:4). It is also a purchased blessing of Christ's atonement, as all blessings in the Christian life must be. However, regeneration is also *the cause of* our being united to Christ by faith. The important point for our map is that regeneration precedes faith. Our faith union is a result of our regeneration. To put it plainly, the common way of thinking about this – that we believe in order to be born again – is backward. We do not believe in order to be born again; we are born again in order to believe.

This follows from all that we have said stemming from our anchor texts, John 3 and Ephesians 2. The redemption of Christ, accomplished once and for all, is applied by the Spirit of God working effectually in the lives of those Christ came to save. Nature cannot rise above nature. Sinful flesh cannot produce faith. The sinner who is dead in trespasses and sins cannot produce faith. Therefore, the importance of seeing that regeneration is what leads to faith is that it guards the God-centred, God-exalting concept of salvation taught in the Scriptures. It also takes seriously the depravity of fallen sinners. And it keeps us as sinners from the pride-inducing thought that salvation is somehow in our hands and that we can produce faith at will. Indeed, we cannot, and we do not have a will to believe until the Holy

Spirit grants that faith in his effectual work in our souls. There can be an experiential bond between God and the sinner only by faith; and that faith is the gift of God.

In regeneration, considered in the narrow sense, the sinner is passive. The Holy Spirit is the sole agent in producing life. We cannot bring ourselves to new birth any more than we could give ourselves life and birth in our mothers' wombs. Or, to put it another way, spiritually dead sinners cannot raise themselves from the dead any more than Lazarus could have raised himself from the tomb. The graces that follow regeneration necessarily follow, and do not precede, this stupendous life-giving work of God's Spirit. Even though we believe, faith is not something we have produced ourselves.

Therefore, it is a very serious and God-dishonouring error to fail to see that our eternal, elective union with Christ is the foundation for our faith union. It also means that the order of salvation and how we think of it is important for preaching and Christian living. If we think we can produce faith ourselves, that robs the Saviour of his glory. It ascribes to us what should be ascribed to God alone. If, on the other hand, our souls are lovingly gripped by the reality that regeneration is entirely of God's grace and that faith is God's gift, we will be led into a life of gratitude and service, consciously giving glory to God for it all. The order could never be faith leading to regeneration; it must be regeneration that produces faith.

Regeneration, then, grants and produces faith. In faith we embrace Christ as Lord and Saviour of our lives.

Regeneration is necessary so that Christ and his benefits do not remain outside of us! Calvin was profoundly right in his observation which we quoted earlier: 'as long as Christ remains outside of us, and we are separated from him, all that he has suffered and done for the salvation of the human race remains useless and of no value to us.'

The sovereign will of God

The logical priority of regeneration over faith means that salvation does not originate with us, but in the sovereign will of God. Why does one person believe and not another? The answer can only be traced to God's sovereign will (cf. Matt. 11:25-27). This is necessary to raise us up to the heights of praise, but also to take us down to the depths of confessing that our salvation is of the Lord and not of us. In this way Christ is exalted, and we are properly humbled.

An experiential reality

Let us be careful: of course it is very important to get our thinking right about these things! But one can think the right things and still not have warm, vital hearts towards God. Perhaps the best way to understand this wonderful truth of union with Christ to which we are introduced by regeneration is by the analogy of marriage, biblically understood. When a man and a woman are united in holy matrimony they remain distinct, yet become one. She takes her husband's name. Her husband will protect, love and nourish her. She will honour and obey him. The two are one in blessings, trials, plans, purpose and heart. What is legally his is now hers; what is hers is his. Moreover, when a woman is married to her husband, this is the new and determinative reality. There was a ceremony of union. It would be ridiculous for the bride to say, 'This has nothing to do with me, it has no impact on my life.' On the contrary, life can never be the same again! So our union with Christ was accomplished in Christ's death and resurrection. In regeneration God gives us the gift of faith by which we are bound experientially to Christ like a bride to her husband. This union truly changes us, our hearts, everything! Just as the calling of the wife is to realize in concrete ways her union with her husband as she lives out of that union, so in the Christian life, every day and in every way we live in, for and out of the Christ with whom we are united. All of our goals centre on the Christ who rules on the throne. All of our thoughts and affections are now turned Christ-ward (Col. 3:1–4). Here is the secret to communion with Christ, the whisper of daily grace in our ears, the calm in the storm and the present experience of future hope. Regeneration that brings about such life-giving union is no small thing. Let us be glad if we have experienced it.

10

Calling, Regeneration and Conversion

The map of salvation which we saw in the last chapter leads us to an essential principle. It is not popular to hold high and consistent views of the sovereignty of God over all things and, especially, the doctrine of salvation; but, if we are truly born again, we will increasingly want to exalt the Lord and not ourselves. The essential principle in the Reformed *ordo salutis* is to exalt God in the sovereignty of salvation. The nineteenth-century English Baptist preacher C. H. Spurgeon put it well:

> Calvinism means the placing of the eternal God at the head of all things. I look at everything through its relation to God's glory. I see God first, and man far down the list. We think too much of God to please this age.[1]

---

[1] Quoted by Iain H. Murray, *The Forgotten Spurgeon* (Edinburgh: Banner of Truth Trust, 2009), p. 198. By 'Calvinsim' Spurgeon simply means the theology of grace found in the Bible and preached by the Protestant Reformers and their heirs.

A denial or minimization of God's sovereignty in regenerating sinners exalts man rather than God. From first to last, salvation is of grace. It is noteworthy that a fruit of the new birth is a desire to glorify God. Jonathan Edwards records that from his childhood he saw the sovereignty of God to be a 'horrible doctrine.' But, after his conversion, he saw the beauty of God's sovereignty and confessed: 'Absolute sovereignty is what I love to ascribe to God.'[1] Everything was new for him and he found 'sweet' the glory and majesty of God which once he had found bitter.

With the beautiful truth of the sovereignty of God in the salvation of sinners in mind, let us now zoom out somewhat and look at the relationship between calling, regeneration and conversion.

Calling, general and special

As we look at what the Scriptures say about God's call in salvation, it becomes clear that we must distinguish between 'general' and 'special' or 'effectual' calling. The distinction is not between the content of the call, which is the same in both instances, but in God's intention to make the call effective in one case and not in another. The same gospel is preached to those God has chosen from eternity as well as to those who have not been chosen (Matt. 28:28–30) – though it is not applied with saving power to all but only to God's elect at the time he has purposed to make it effective in their lives.

[1] Jonathan Edwards, 'Memoirs,' in *The Works of Jonathan Edwards* (Edinburgh: Banner of Truth Trust, 1974), vol. 1, pp. xii–xiii.

Suppose two sinners come into a worship service together. Imagine that they are brothers, indeed, identical twins. They are remarkably similar. They shared the same home environment. They have the same likes and dislikes. But, as they sit under the preaching of the word, one believes and the other does not. In fact, the one who does not believe is actually hostile to the message. What made the difference? It was not their free will but God's free grace. The Holy Spirit regenerated one and did not regenerate the other. The general call of the gospel went out to both; but the call was made effectual only to one. The one who did not respond did not do so because of his sin and is fully responsible for his failure to repent. The one who did respond in faith came to Christ only because of the regeneration of the Holy Spirit and not because of anything within him. He did not come because he was better, or because he was more inclined to believe than his twin. Both twins were depraved in the totality of their being and incapable of responding in their own strength to the preaching of Christ. The twins were spiritually dead in trespasses and sins. But one of them was raised to life by the call of God the Father through the Holy Spirit who applied the work of Christ to his soul. One was called effectually as God granted faith and repentance as a free gift. Behind this effectual call is the eternal, electing decree of God. Paul expresses this clearly when he says:

> For those whom he foreknew [God] also predestined to be
> conformed to the image of his Son, in order that he might

be the firstborn among many brothers. And those whom he predestined he also called, and those whom he called he also justified, and those whom he justified he also glorified (Rom. 8:29, 30).

Or as Luke records in Acts, 'as many as were appointed to eternal life believed' (Acts 13:48).

The Dutch theologian Wilhelmus à Brakel compared the 'free will' approach to what transpires in a race. The prize is on display at the end. 'The acquisition of the prize, however, is contingent upon the runners themselves.' In this way the distinction between the external call and the effectual call is removed 'in order to protect the idol of man's own ability.'[1] The Scriptures, however, teach something very different, and this is à Brakel's point. The dead sinner must be brought to life (Eph. 2:1, 2), he must be born again (John 3:3, 7), he must be drawn by God (John 6:44), his heart must be opened as was Lydia's when she came to faith (Acts 16:14). The sinner cannot respond to the call of God in his own strength and ability. To use à Brakel's illustration, he cannot run the race and acquire the prize. If we are Christians, how our souls should be moved to praise as we consider that the Lord calls us, even though we were not in any way more deserving than another!

Calling and regeneration

What is the relationship between God's general call and the regenerating work of the Holy Spirit? God's call becomes

[1] Wilhelmus à Brakel, *The Christian's Reasonable Service* (Ligonier, PA: Soli Deo Gloria, 1993), vol. 2, p. 194.

effectual the moment regeneration has taken place. Regeneration and God's internal call are virtually synonymous. A sinner's response to the internal call shows that regeneration has taken place. Jesus follows his proclamation of the new birth in John 3 with the message of the response of faith (John 3:16ff.). The call of God, when effectual, is the call to faith in Christ. Sinners are drawn by the Father (John 6:44) and called according to God's purpose (Rom. 8:28). Regeneration enables the sinner to respond to the call of God the Father. It is a wonderful opening of that person's heart (Acts 16:14).

At this point, it is once again necessary to guard against a misunderstanding. Frequently, people misrepresent the scriptural, Reformed understanding of this issue by suggesting that the Lord brings us to himself against our wills. This is not correct. While it is true that those who come to know Christ had no will to do so prior to their regeneration and effectual call, regeneration changes their will so that the sinner not only must come, not only will come, but also actually *desires* to come to Christ. Sinners never come to the Lord against their wills; rather, they are made willing in the day of God's power (Psa. 110:3).

> The Lord does not compel the will, but the Lord grants the intellect eyes to perceive the spiritual dimension of spiritual things, and by means of that light the Lord penetrates the will and inclines it to embrace the matters with which it is now acquainted and finds desirable. The Lord thus engages both the intellect and the will.[1]

[1] à Brakel, *The Christian's Reasonable Service*, vol. 2, p. 210.

The Lord, then, gives to sinners a new disposition of the heart, a new way of seeing, a new desire, a renewed understanding and a renewed will. Paul could continue to pray for a deepening of such things in the hearts of the Ephesians because, as the Lord raises sinners from spiritual death, he grants these new dispositions, desires and directions. So Paul's desire for the Christians in Ephesus was that

> the God of our Lord Jesus Christ, the Father of glory, may give you a spirit of wisdom and of revelation in the knowledge of him, having the eyes of your hearts enlightened, that you may know what is the hope to which he has called you, what are the riches of his glorious inheritance in the saints, and what is the immeasurable greatness of his power towards us who believe, according to the working of his great might that he worked in Christ when he raised him from the dead and seated him at his right hand in the heavenly places (Eph. 1:17–20).

Sinners have no natural desire for communion with God, no natural desire or ability to believe and repent. 'No man can come to me, except the Father which hath sent me draw him' (John 6:44, AV). The Lord alone can enlighten the eyes (Eph. 1:18), he alone can remove the heart of stone and give a heart of flesh (Ezek. 36:26). At the moment of regeneration, sinners are passive. Indeed, they are very active in opposing God; but they are passive in the sense that they cannot produce within themselves the change of disposition necessary to come into fellowship with the Lord.

Jonathan Edwards rightly saw regeneration as a radical and universal change from a sinner to a saint so that the person now has 'new principles of perception and action.' He now has 'a new principle of understanding,' 'eyes to see' and a new principle of 'will and inclination.' Indeed, 'the man now loves God, and loves Christ, which he could not love before. He relishes holiness and holy and heavenly things, which he could not relish before.'[1] Edwards rightly speaks of a new sense of things. The regenerate sinner not only has a rational understanding that God is glorious but 'he has a sense of the gloriousness of God in his heart.' Edwards compares it to the difference between a man who has a rational sense of the sweetness of honey and the one who has actually tasted the sweetness of honey.[2]

To alter the illustration just a little, suppose a chemist has analysed peppermint and can tell you all about its chemical make-up, but has never tasted it. Another person has no idea about the chemistry behind peppermint but has tasted it for himself and delights in its sweetness. The latter has experienced peppermint but the chemist has not. So it is with the new birth. Those who are born again 'believe the doctrines of God's Word to be divine, because they see divinity in them,' says Edwards. 'They see a divine, and transcendent, and most evidently distinguishing glory in them; such a glory as, if clearly seen, does not leave room

---

[1] Jonathan Edwards, 'Born Again,' in *The Works of Jonathan Edwards* (Edinburgh: Banner of Truth Trust, 1974), vol. 2, p. 14.

[2] Jonathan Edwards, 'A Divine and Supernatural Light,' in *Works*, vol. 2, p. 14.

to doubt of their being of God, and not of men.'[1] Most important in Edwards' observations is the recognition that the new sense of things brought about by regeneration carries with it an apprehension of the loveliness and beauty of holiness and grace rather than a mere opinion that God is holy. In addition, the excellency of God and of Christ and his method of redemption captivates the soul. This new man does not

> merely rationally believe that God is glorious, but he has a sense of the gloriousness of God in his heart. There is not only a rational belief that God is holy, and that holiness is a good thing; but there is a sense of the loveliness of God's holiness. There is not only a speculative judging that God is gracious, but a sense of how amiable God is upon that account; or a sense of the beauty of this divine attribute.[2]

Jonathan Edwards can help us think more deeply about the changes the new birth brings to those who experience it. In a sermon entitled 'Love More Excellent Than the Extraordinary Gifts of the Spirit' he points out that when the Holy Spirit bestows saving grace, 'He imparts himself to the soul in his own holy nature.'[3] Those who experience new birth become, therefore, spiritual beings. We then, who are born again, for the first time have a spiritual sense and perceive God in his grandeur and beauty – a thing

---

[1] Edwards, 'A Divine and Supernatural Light,' *Works*, vol. 2, p. 14.

[2] Edwards, 'A Divine and Supernatural Light,' *Works*, vol. 2, p. 14.

[3] Jonathan Edwards, 'Love More Excellent than the Extraordinary Gifts of the Spirit,' in *Charity and Its Fruits* (Edinburgh: Banner of Truth Trust, 1982), p. 36.

impossible to the natural mind. And, since we are indwelt by the Holy Spirit, we now – astounding thought! – enter into the love of the three persons of the Trinity. 'That principle in the soul of the saints, which is the grand Christian virtue, and which is the soul and essence and summary comprehension of all grace, is a principle of divine love.'[1] Only eternity will open our eyes to the grandeur of the Spirit's work in our hearts that would make us partakers of the love experienced in the relations of the three persons of the Holy Trinity.

Regeneration, conviction of sin and adult conversion

Since regeneration is an instantaneous transition from death to life, brought about by the Holy Spirit, it is obvious that no sinners in and of themselves may prepare themselves for it. As quoted earlier, the Westminster Confession states in 9.3:

> Man, by his fall into a state of sin, hath wholly lost all ability of will to any spiritual good accompanying salvation: so as, a natural man, being altogether averse from that good, and dead in sin, is not able, by his own strength, to convert himself, or to prepare himself thereunto.

Similarly, the Canons of Dordt, under the third and fourth heads of doctrine, Article 3, state:

> Therefore all men are conceived in sin, and by nature children of wrath, incapable of saving good, prone to evil,

---

[1] Jonathan Edwards, 'Treatise on Grace,' in *The Works of Jonathan Edwards* (New Haven: Yale University Press, 2003), vol. 21, pp. 166ff.

dead in sin, and in bondage thereto, and without the regenerating grace of the Holy Spirit, they are neither able nor
willing to return to God, to reform the depravity of their
nature, or to dispose themselves to reformation.

While affirming that a sinner cannot bring himself to
saving faith, we recognize the relationship between the
Spirit's regenerating work and his use of the preaching of
God's word. The preaching of God's law and of his judgment to come are means of evangelism largely neglected
by the church in our day. But how can men be saved if they
do not understand that they are lost? This raises a further
question: when a sinner sees himself to be a sinner, when
the law of God convicts a sinner who comes to faith in
Christ, is that conviction prior to – in a sense a preparation for – regeneration, or has regeneration already taken
place? Take, for example, this quotation from a sermon by
the great eighteenth-century American preacher Samuel
Davies:

> If ever you have sought shelter under [Christ's] wings, you
> have seen your sins, the curses of the law, and the powers
> of hell, as it were, hovering over you, and ready to seize and
> devour you as their prey. You have been made deeply sen-
> sible, that Jesus alone was able to save you. You found you
> could not shelter yourselves under the covert of your own
> righteousness, and were constrained to give up all hopes of
> saving yourselves by any thing you could do in your own
> strength. Hereupon, as perishing, helpless creatures, you
> have cast yourselves entirely upon the protection of Jesus
> Christ, and put your souls into his hands, to be saved by

him in his own way: and you have also submitted freely to his authority, willing to be ruled and disposed of entirely according to his pleasure.[1]

True, saving conviction leads to a conscious act of faith in Christ alone for salvation. A sinner, in other words, cannot see himself truly to be a sinner in need of a Saviour apart from the life-giving work of the Holy Spirit.

Much may precede conversion that the Lord may and has purposed to use. In God's providence people may read the Gospel of John and later the Spirit may use it for their conversion. A child may hear the sweep of Bible history in family worship and Sunday school but only think seriously about such things later in life as the Spirit uses them to convict and to convert. There is a wonderful story told of an old farmer in colonial Virginia by the name of Luke Short who was converted at the ripe old age of one hundred when reflecting on some words he had heard from the lips of the Puritan minister John Flavel some eighty-five years earlier when he was just a young lad in Dartmouth, England. The old farmer did nothing to prepare himself for salvation; rather, the Lord went before him in the hearing of the word. As Bavinck says,

> These operations and experiences themselves do not include regeneration, but nevertheless according to God's leading they often precede regeneration – and thus constitute preceding, but not preparatory, operations!

[1] Samuel Davies, *Sermons of Samuel Davies* (New York: Robert Carter & Bros, 1858), vol. 2, p. 332.

Deaf persons cannot hear, but under and in connection with the external calling, God can make them hear. Dead persons cannot rise up, but by means of the Word, God can sow the seed of life in their hearts, so that with the prodigal son they rise up and return to the Father. In all these cases the connection between regeneration and calling is maintained, as is the connection between the operation of the Spirit and the administration of the Word.[1]

Bavinck's thought is that sinners cannot qualify themselves beforehand to receive the gospel – this is what he means by the phrase 'preparatory operations.' Instead, the Lord goes ahead of a man to plant the seed that the Spirit will germinate.

Dr Martyn Lloyd-Jones saw clearly the error of supposing that the preaching of the law in evangelism was a kind of preparation on man's part for salvation. No! The Lord has ordained the preaching of the law and the judgment to come. Iain H. Murray summarizes this crucial theme in Lloyd-Jones' preaching:

There is a work of God in the unconverted preparatory to their seeing their need of faith in Christ. Sinners need to be 'awakened,' not in order to be qualified for salvation, nor to 'prepare themselves' (a thing Puritans were wrongly accused of believing) but because it is God's general method to bring men to faith by first causing them to know their need of Christ.

---

[1] Bavinck, *Saved By Grace: The Holy Spirit's Work in Calling and Regeneration* (Grand Rapids: Reformation Heritage, 2008), pp. 98–99.

Murray quotes in this context the clarifying statement of nineteenth-century Scottish theologian John Duncan: 'God needs to do a great deal *to* sinners in order to turn them; but God is requiring nothing *of* sinners but that they return.'[1]

You may be reading this but as yet do not know Christ as Lord and Saviour. Perhaps you grew up in a Christian home or under a faithful minister of God's word, but have not yet come to Christ for salvation. It is the Lord's way to plant a seed by one minister, to water it by another and to make it grow in his own time (1 Cor. 3:6). May the Holy Spirit enable you to heed the external call of the gospel by granting internal saving power. 'If you confess with your mouth that Jesus is Lord and believe in your heart that God raised him from the dead, you will be saved' (Rom. 10:9).

[1] Iain H. Murray, *D. Martyn Lloyd-Jones: The Fight of Faith, 1939–1981* (Edinburgh: Banner of Truth Trust, 1990), p. 723.

11

The Consequences of the New Birth: Faith and Repentance

The word 'regeneration' means 'to begin again.' When a sinner is regenerated, that person is given a new start. Regeneration results in a radical change in how that person thinks and lives because God has given him a renewed nature. Paul speaks of this in 2 Corinthians 5:17: 'Therefore, if anyone is in Christ, he is a new creation. The old has passed away; behold, the new has come.' When the Spirit regenerates the sinner, that person now belongs to the age to come. Everything is now new for him; nothing looks the same as it did before. Before this, God's word was a sealed book for him, but now it pulses with life as he reads and finds his Saviour on every page. This change is what Martin Luther experienced when he came to faith and understood the justice of God and his acceptance in Christ: 'Thereupon I felt myself to be reborn and to have gone through open doors into paradise.'[1] Indeed, this is

Roland H. Bainton, *Here I Stand* (Nashville: Abingdon, 1978), p. 49.

precisely what had happened. Luther now participated in the resurrection life of Christ (Phil. 3:10, 11) by the Spirit's regeneration and had been granted saving faith by the Holy Spirit. He now belonged to the age to come; his citizenship was in heaven (Phil. 3:20). Through the new birth sinners experience 'the washing of regeneration and renewal of the Holy Spirit' (Titus 3:5), come to participate in Christ and also begin to experience the age to come.

It needs to be stressed that when regeneration happens, a profound change takes place. If the new birth has taken place, or, to use Paul's language, a person has been raised spiritually from the dead, it makes no sense to claim that this does not change how a person thinks or acts. How can a sinner's nature have been renewed and it not make a visible difference in his life? There must be consequences. The immediate consequences of regeneration are faith and repentance.

Saving faith

When a sinner is renewed by the Holy Spirit he is granted saving faith. Sinners themselves are passive in the sense that they can do nothing to bring themselves to this new life. But the moment they are born again, they are granted saving faith. In personal experience, regeneration and faith cannot be distinguished; faith is produced by the regenerating work of the Holy Spirit. The first exercise of faith is the immediate consequence of the Holy Spirit's regeneration.

Jesus speaks of this as knowing God (John 17:3). In 1 John 4:7, 8 the Apostle John links regeneration (God's action) with knowing God (the consequence): 'Whoever loves has been born of God and knows God. Anyone who does not love does not know God, because God is love.' A sinner's heart is cleansed in regeneration (Ezek. 36:25–27; 1 Cor. 6:11; Titus 3:5). His will is set free to embrace Jesus Christ, and his affections are no longer focused on self but on Christ. If this change is real, it will be visible in a genuine change of life.

What, precisely, does this renewing work of the Holy Spirit in granting saving faith enable the sinner to do? The Spirit of God enables the sinner to trust in Christ, to embrace him in a way that leads to salvation. Indeed, the New Testament speaks of believing 'into' union with Christ. Saving faith, therefore, involves three elements: knowledge, assent and, most importantly, trust or reliance upon Christ alone for salvation. This is the fruit of regeneration. As our anchor texts teach, the sinner is born again in order to believe (John 3:5, 14ff.). The dead sinner is raised in Christ and now believes in Christ as a result of spiritual resurrection (Eph. 2:1, 4–8). Faith in Christ is God's gift (Phil. 1:29). Sinners can believe only through grace (Acts 18:27).

In order to grow in your understanding of these things, I encourage you to turn to volume 5 of the Works of John Owen, which is one of the most, if not the most, important books on the theme of justification by faith. Chapter 15 unpacks what faith alone in Christ means. Even though his language and writing style are often challenging, it is well worth one's effort! Owen points to the following five characteristics of the faith that alone justifies – this faith which is the fruit of regeneration:

1. It is a *receiving* faith.
2. It is a *looking* faith.
3. It is a *coming-unto-Christ* faith.
4. It is a *fleeing-for-refuge* faith.
5. It is a *leaning-on-God* faith.

In justifying faith, Owen summarizes,

> Convinced sinners do wholly go out of themselves to rest
> upon God in Christ for mercy, pardon, life, righteousness,
> and salvation.[1]

Regarding the relationship between regeneration and faith as its fruit, consider this as well: we have stressed all along with Scripture and in light of our foundation texts, John 3 and Ephesians 2, that regeneration is God's unique and sovereign work. But it is important to note also that this stress upon God's sovereignty is one of the reasons why we genuinely come to know the Lord by faith. Faith is God's gift and not something we manufacture ourselves. We believe, but God enables us to believe.

Jonathan Edwards powerfully brought this out in his sermon 'God Glorified in Man's Dependence.' Here he showed that one reason why we come to the Lord by *faith* is to acknowledge total dependence on the Lord. It is fitting that faith 'be required of all, in order to their having the benefit of this redemption, that they should be sensible of, and acknowledge this dependence on God for it.' Indeed,

---

[1] John Owen, *The Doctrine of Justification by Faith*, in *Works of John Owen* (Edinburgh: Banner of Truth Trust, 2007), vol. 5, pp. 290–294.

says Edwards, it is 'the delight of a believing soul to abase itself and exalt God alone.'[1] When the sinner is called to believe in Christ, not only is human responsibility stressed but, more so, the sovereignty of the God who alone can grant saving faith. We believe in Christ, but that faith simply receives what God alone can offer. Faith contributes nothing; it is merely the empty hand that receives the gift. In the language of the Reformers, the grace of saving faith is the 'alone' instrument of justification.

Evangelical repentance

The twin sister of saving faith is evangelical, or gospel-driven, repentance. When the Holy Spirit regenerates and grants saving faith he also grants repentance. Faith and repentance are distinguishable, but inseparable. The one is never found without the other. Regeneration is a radical transformation of the sinner; therefore, one will see a radical change of direction in the sinner who comes to Christ. Of the several terms used in the Bible for repentance, the main Greek term, *metanoia*, indicates a change of mind or purpose. Repentance means that the sinner now returns to the God from whom he had departed. True repentance is not simply

---

[1] Jonathan Edwards, 'God Glorified in Man's Dependence,' in *The Works of Jonathan Edwards* (Edinburgh: Banner of Truth Trust, 1974), vol. 2, p. 7. In the preface to the first edition of the publication of this sermon (an appendix in the Yale edition), Thomas Prince and William Cooper wrote: 'if these which we call the doctrines of grace ever come to be contemned or disrelished, vital piety will proportionably languish and wear away, as these doctrines always sink in the esteem of men, upon the decay of serious religion.' *The Works of Jonathan Edwards* (New Haven: Yale University Press, 1999), vol. 17, p. 215.

regret and sorrow for shameful deeds (2 Cor. 7:10) but, as Bavinck beautifully put it, consists of

> an inner breaking of the heart (Psa. 51:19 and Acts 2:37), or a grief because of sin itself, because it is in conflict with God's will and provokes His wrath, and of a sincere remorse and a hating and fleeing of sin.

Bavinck points to the prodigal son in Luke's Gospel (Luke 15:18) who 'dares to go to the Father and to confess his sins before His face because in the depths of his heart he believes that the Father is his Father.'[1]

In granting repentance the Holy Spirit makes use of God's word as it is read and preached (Psa. 19:7; Acts 2:10, 11). Repentance often comes as the result of the Holy Spirit's bringing God's law home to the regenerate sinner in a spiritually penetrating way (Rom. 7:7). However, the law's spirituality is seen not only by reading the commandments and perceiving one's failure and need of grace, but in other ways. For example, a sinner might hear a sermon about the love of the cross and find in the sacrifice of Christ convicting and converting power impressed upon his soul, seeing the price paid in love for sinners to deliver them from the curse of the law (Gal. 3:10). In every case, however, sinners are confronted to varying degrees with a view of God in his majesty and holiness (Isa. 6; Job 42:5, 6; Psa. 130:4). To preach God's law rightly the preacher must preach the cross in relation to the law; to preach the cross

---

[1] Herman Bavinck, *Our Reasonable Faith* (Grand Rapids: Baker, 1980), p. 437.

rightly the minister must also preach the law, since holiness is most gloriously manifested there. In other words, to understand the spirituality of the law is to be driven out of self and to Christ.

When the Holy Spirit regenerates a soul and grants the grace of repentance, this repentance differs from every other form of 'repentance' that preceded regeneration. Scottish pastor John Colquhoun (1748–1827) in his book on this very subject gathers together the Bible's teaching on repentance, showing first of all that true repentance must be distinguished from what he calls 'natural' repentance. All sinners can, from time to time, have a natural sorrow for going against their consciences. This is a long way from true repentance. Equally, 'legal' repentance is not true repentance. This man fears because he has violated the law of God, realizing to some extent that his sins deserve God's wrath. But the legalist is not sorry that he has offended God and transgressed his law; rather, he is sorry that the law is so strict and inflexible. His love for sin and hatred of holiness are unchanged. True repentance granted by the sovereign work of God's Spirit is 'evangelical,' that is, 'gospel,' repentance. It is, says Colquhoun,

> A gracious principle and habit implanted in the soul by the Spirit of Christ, in the exercise of which a regenerate and believing sinner, deeply sensible of the exceeding sinfulness and just demerit of his innumerable sins, is truly humbled and grieved before the Lord, on account of the sinfulness and hurtfulness of them. He feels bitter remorse, unfeigned sorrow, and deep self-abhorrence for the aggravated trans-

gressions of his life, and the deep depravity of his nature; chiefly, because by all his innumerable provocations he has dishonoured an infinitely holy and gracious God, transgressed a law which is 'holy, and just, and good,' and defiled, deformed, and even destroyed his own precious soul. This godly sorrow for sin and this holy abhorrence of it arise from a spiritual discovery of pardoning mercy with God in Christ, and from the exercise of trusting his mercy. And these feelings and exercises are always accompanied by an unfeigned love of universal holiness, and by fixed resolutions and endeavours to turn from all iniquity to God and to walk before him in newness of life.[1]

It is important to point out that faith and repentance continue throughout the Christian life. Every day the Christian believes and repents and cries out 'Convert me, that I may be converted' (see Jer. 31:18). The first of Martin Luther's Ninety-Five Theses nailed on the church door at Wittenberg in 1517 was intended to distinguish repentance from penance. Here Luther pointed out the ongoing relationship of repentance to Christian living: 'When our Lord and Master Jesus Christ, said, "Repent" [Matt. 4:17], he willed the entire life of believers to be one of repentance.'[2] The truly regenerate sinner will genuinely repent, and will continue so to do. The standard that determines

---

[1] John Colquhoun, *Repentance* (Edinburgh: Banner of Truth Trust, 2010), pp. 2, 3.

[2] Martin Luther, 'Explanations of the Ninety-Five Theses,' in Luther's *Works* (Philadelphia: Fortress Press, 1957), pp. 31, 83. The posting of the Ninety-Five Theses was the unforeseen beginning of the Protestant Reformation.

our initial and ongoing repentance is the law of God. This, then, points us to another essential fruit of regeneration: love for the law of God.

The law of God now loved

Before coming to Christ, the law of God was our enemy because we were enemies to it. In our rebellion we made our sinfulness worse by constant transgression of God's law both inwardly and outwardly. But it is especially important to note, in the context of doctrine which claims to be Bible-based, that a truly regenerate person now has a different attitude towards the law of God. The Lord Jesus died to remove the curse of the law (Gal. 3:10). On the basis of Christ's satisfying the demands of divine justice (Rom. 3:21–25) the condemnation of God's law has been removed and the believer in Christ is freed from its curse. However, it does not stop there. The law, which is 'holy and righteous and good' (Rom. 7:12) since it is a reflection of God's own nature, is now the Christian's delight. God's law is now the regenerate believer's friend. The Holy Spirit who grants saving faith and repentance promises in the new covenant to write the law upon the believer's heart (Jer. 31:33; Heb. 8:6, 8–13; 10:16). Not only is the law's condemnation now removed, but the regenerated and believing heart is no longer at enmity with God and his law. Therefore, the law written on the heart by the Holy Spirit in his sovereign, regenerating work becomes our friend, our standard and guide for ongoing Christian living and sanctification. Any approach to the Christian life that minimizes the role of the law of God as the Christian's friend and guide is simply out of accord with the Bible's teaching. Unhappily, there have always been those who say that salvation by grace does away with any concern for the law of God.

Any approach to the Christian life that sets aside God's law as a guide is faulty, for two reasons. First, the assumption that one might be born again and have true faith in Christ and yet have no concern for holy living denies Christ's Lordship in our lives. That viewpoint is, very sadly, all too prevalent. However, this assumes that one can receive Christ in his office as priest but reject him as prophet and king. This cannot be; one cannot receive a divided Christ. When someone receives Christ he receives the whole Christ, the Christ who rules and reigns over and within us by his word and Spirit, and directs us by his law.

But, also, the 'antinomian'[1] error that we have been describing fails to realize the ongoing relevance of God's law and that the so-called third use of the law – to guide and direct Christian living – is, as Calvin recognized, its principal use. Calvin recognized that the Bible clearly teaches that the law not only convicts sinners of their sin and guilt before God, but continues to guide and direct Christians in their new life. The truly regenerate believer longs to obey God. Calvin beautifully stresses this in his *Institutes of the Christian Religion*. Calvin's wisdom and balance and, most of all, scriptural understanding with respect to the law of God in the believer's life are striking.

---

[1] A technical term meaning to be 'against the law' or moral norms.

He recognized that the law 'may no longer condemn and destroy [believers'] consciences by frightening and confounding them.'[1] But believers benefit from the law which is now their friend. As it teaches the nature of God's will and as we meditate upon the law we are 'aroused to obedience ... strengthened in it, and ... drawn back from the slippery path of transgression.'[2] In our ongoing struggle to live out of the fullness of our regenerated life we must have the law as our friendly guide to show us the way in which we ought to go. Hear Calvin's encouragement once more. He urges Christians not to be frightened of using the law in their daily walk:

> For the law is not now acting toward us as a rigorous enforcement officer who is not satisfied unless the requirements are met. But in this perfection to which it exhorts us, the law points out the goal toward which throughout life we are to strive. In this the law is no less profitable than consistent with our duty. If we fail not in this struggle, it is well. Indeed, this whole life is a race [see 1 Cor. 9:24–26]; when its course has been run, the Lord will grant us to attain the goal to which our efforts now press forward from afar.[3]

The Christian is moved to live by the Spirit in gratitude to God for redemption. This is a powerful, motivating gratitude that longs to love and live by the law of God that is now written upon our hearts. Anything less fails to see

---

[1] Calvin, *Institutes*, II.vii.14.

[2] Calvin, *Institutes*, II.vii.12.

[3] Calvin, *Institutes*, II.vii.13.

that living life by God's law is a part of our new-found freedom in Christ, for freedom must have direction (Gal. 5:13). Obedience to the law of God is the fruit of the Spirit's regeneration. We obey *because* we have been accepted, not *in order* to be accepted. Therefore, unchastity, immodesty, stealing, Sabbath-breaking, and all else that is contrary to God's law is also contrary to our regenerate natures, our hearts, upon which in regeneration the law of God has been written. If you are a believer, do not be taken in by any movement describing itself as a 'grace movement' that sets aside the central place of the law of God as the Christian's guide to holy living. A truly gracious heart loves the law of the Lord. A deep understanding of and commitment to the simple statement of the Puritan Samuel Bolton would bring untold blessing into the church of our day: 'The law sends us to the gospel for our justification; the gospel sends us to the law to frame our way of life.'[1]

A number of years ago I was speaking to a group of young people in a church. The questions coming from some of them could be summarized in this way: 'How close can I come to sin and not sin?' Frankly, I have had that experience more than once. Sinners want the benefits of Christ without the Lordship of Christ. But those who are truly born again learn that the call of God is to keep as far away from sin as possible. Instead, they learn to love God's law more and more, use it as their guide and say within their

---

[1] Samuel Bolton, *The True Bounds of Christian Freedom* (Edinburgh: Banner of Truth Trust, 1978), p. 11.

hearts, 'How far away can we get from all temptation and sin, from whatever displeases the Lord?' This stress upon hatred of sin and loving the law is one crying need of the church in our day.

We began this chapter with the delightful observation that 'regeneration' means a new beginning. Perhaps as you read this the Holy Spirit is enabling you to see that this indeed has been your need all along. When your needy heart trusts Jesus Christ, you will see that all things are indeed new. You will have saving faith in Christ, a new heart of repentance and a love for the law of God under which you were formerly condemned.

12

What Happens to Infants and Children?

Perhaps, next to the doctrine of the Trinity, regeneration raises some of the most mysterious and difficult questions with which we have to grapple. For example, the relationship between regeneration and preaching and the relationship between conviction of sin and conversion are difficult to grasp. Among these mysteries also belongs the question of the regeneration of infants and small children. Knowing more about these difficulties and their biblical solutions, insofar as God has revealed them, will deepen our amazement at the saving operations of the Holy Spirit in the lives of his people.

The regeneration of infants and young children

Infants may indeed be born again by the Holy Spirit who works when, how and where he pleases. John the Baptist was regenerated from his mother's womb (Luke 1:15, 44) and Jeremiah was set apart from the womb (Jer. 1:5). The Bible speaks of God's special favour towards the children of believing parents (1 Cor. 7:14), and those who are chosen of God will be regenerated and saved. It is often the case that children who grow up in the context of the word of God, as did Timothy (2 Tim. 3:15), show evidence of saving faith at an early age. One of the elders of the congregation where I minister cannot tell you when or where he first believed. He simply says that he cannot remember a time when he did not know and love the Lord Jesus Christ. This is not because he did not need regenerating! His testimony is, simply, that the Lord worked so tenderly, yet powerfully, in his infancy or early childhood that he does not know when the transition from wrath to grace took place. Wilhelmus à Brakel serves as another example. He feared and loved the Lord from his youth and, though converted, could not tell of a time when the conversion had taken place.[1]

This is the testimony of many who are brought up in Christian or covenant families. A particularly interesting example of the conversion of a young child is recorded by Jonathan Edwards in his *Narrative of Surprising Conversions*.[2] Phebe Bartlett was four years old in 1735 when the Lord began to work in her heart, even though her parents thought that because she was so young she was incapable of understanding the gospel. A conversation with her brother greatly altered her and she began spending time in secret

---

[1] Dr W. Fieret and Wilhelmus à Brakel, in Wilhelmus à Brakel, *The Christian's Reasonable Service* (Ligonier, PA: Soli Deo Gloria, 1992), vol. 1, p. xxxii.

[2] Jonathan Edwards, 'A Narrative of Surprising Conversions,' in *Jonathan Edwards on Revival* (Edinburgh: Banner of Truth Trust, 1987), pp. 63ff.

prayer five or six times a day. She was overheard in earnest prayer, pleading with God for the forgiveness of her sins, until one day she declared to her mother that she had been converted. She said that she loved God better than father, mother and family. She had been afraid of hell, but now declared that she would not be sent there. Her heart was overwhelmed with the desire that others might know the Lord, and it was sensitive to the beauties of the Lord; she wept to consider his great love to her. The fear of God was before her eyes and it showed in various ways. She began strictly to observe the Sabbath, longed to go to worship to hear Jonathan Edwards preach, and loved family and personal worship. She was even greatly upset that she had followed older children to pick plums when she later learned that they had done so without permission. The change in her heart also showed in charity and concern for others and deep compassion for the poor. Was this a passing fancy? No indeed. Famously, a note was added to the publication of the *Narrative*: 'She [Phebe] was living in March, 1789, and maintained the character of a true convert.'

The Lord does, in his sovereignty, regenerate infants and small children. As they grow up in a Christian household, living in the atmosphere of the covenant of grace, regenerated infants believe the gospel presented by father, mother, minister and teachers. The germ of faith belonging to them by virtue of their early regeneration will become obvious through conscious faith with all the fruit of regeneration.

When the infant is regenerated, that infant is converted in the sense that there occurs in the infant mind something which in the rudimentary sphere corresponds to conversion, that is to say, the direction in which the heart and mind – germinal and rudimentary though they be – are turned towards God, towards faith in him, love and obedience to him.[1]

No presumptive regeneration

But a warning is in order. The Lord may regenerate an infant or small child, but that is no justification for the view that is sometimes called 'presumptive regeneration.' It is God's sovereign prerogative to regenerate infants, to give them a heart of faith, so that as they grow they show that they are really and truly converted. But there is nothing in Scripture that tells us to presume upon the regeneration of our children – indeed, it is dangerous and damaging to do so. In some circles it may well be that generations have grown up without hearing the commands of the gospel because of a presumption that children are already regenerated. Presumptive regeneration misperceives the biblical basis for baptizing infants of believers (in churches that believe baptism is for children of believers as well as for adults who have never been baptized before) and the place of children in the covenant of grace, and also fails to grasp the necessity of proclaiming the gospel to children in Christian or covenant families. 'A system for breeding

---

[1] John Murray, 'Regeneration,' in *Collected Writings of John Murray* (Edinburgh: Banner of Truth Trust, 1977), vol. 1, p. 200.

Pharisees, whose cry is "We are Abraham's children," could hardly be better calculated.'[1]

Indeed, the minister of the gospel must approach his congregation knowing that, in most cases, the congregation is mixed. That is, there will be those who know the Lord personally and savingly and those who do not. While those who have a saving knowledge of Christ need to hear preaching and instruction, all the children, young people and adults who live in secret hypocrisy, open rebellion or false assurance must also hear that they are in danger. To them the compassionate call must go forth, 'Have I any pleasure in the death of the wicked, declares the Lord GOD, and not rather that he should turn from his way and live?' (Ezek. 18:23). It is in the context of the gospel freely offered and powerfully preached that many of our young people will come to know Christ in our services of worship, or even in later years, as the Lord applies his word to their hearts, though preached long ago.

No reason to doubt

Another mystery concerns the regeneration of children that die in infancy. What can be more difficult for Christian parents than the death of a child? Are the infants of believers who die in infancy regenerated? Several comments may help us to wrestle with this.

First, infants do not go to heaven because they are sinless. While infants have not committed sin they

---

[1] William Young, 'Historic Calvinism and Neo-Calvinism,' in *Reformed Thought* (Grand Rapids: Reformation Heritage Books, 2011), p. 52.

nevertheless are fallen in Adam and possess a sinful nature. When ministers suggest that infants are saved because they are innocent, this is not Christianity but Pelagianism. All children are fallen in Adam; they are conceived and born in sin. However, believing parents may go to the covenant promise that God is a God to us and to our children (Gen. 17:7; Acts 2:39; 16:31). Paul speaks of the children and unbelieving spouses in families where there is one adult who is born again as being 'holy' (1 Cor. 7:14) by virtue of God's covenant promise. Undoubtedly, it was this covenant promise that comforted David and upon which he relied when he said of his child who died, 'I shall go to him' (2 Sam. 12:15b–23). God made a covenant with Abraham and with his children, and that covenant has never been revoked. 'Believers and their children' does not mean that every child of believers will be saved, but the line of God's electing grace runs through the covenant. However, in the case of infants dying in infancy, when we take into account Jesus' attitude towards covenant children (Matt. 18:14), his words that the kingdom of God belongs to little children (the term used in Luke 18:15–17 means 'infants') and the multitude of souls saved according to Revelation 7:9, the promise of the covenant shines in upon the open grave of the infant. They are not saved because of innocence or deservedness, nor because of sacraments or any reason other than the sovereign grace of God. Our children dying in infancy go to heaven because Christ died for them and the Spirit of God regenerates them, not because they lack a sinful nature. God's grace is greater than our sin. Let every Christian parent take heart from the words of the Canons of Dordt, :

> Since we are to judge the will of God from his Word, which testifies that the children of believers are holy, not by nature, but in virtue of the covenant of grace, in which they together with their parents are comprehended, godly parents have no reason to doubt of the election and salvation of their infant children whom it pleaseth God to call out of this life in their infancy.[1]

---

[1] Canon 1, Article 17.

13

Signs of New Life

When a sinner is born again it will show in a changed life. This should be obvious. Just as a new-born child must grow in self-consciousness and awareness, so regeneration takes place below our consciousness but, where there is birth, there is life and growth. So, when the new birth has been granted to a sinner, that new life will express itself and grow towards maturity. Or, to use the reality of resurrection stressed by Paul, it is impossible for a sinner dead in trespasses and sins to have been raised from the dead yet fail to display this new life. For every true Christian there are certain evidences of new life – marks of being a Christian – that should be apparent.

Using the marks of new birth wisely

The purpose of examining the marks of the Christian life is two-fold. First, they help self-deceived sinners discover the truth about themselves. Not all who say 'Lord, Lord' enter the kingdom of heaven (Matt. 7:21–23). Some rest their eternal hope on an unsound foundation (Matt. 7:24–27).

However, the second use of the marks of a Christian is to deepen the assurance of Christians concerning the Lord's work within them. Though they may have assurance of faith and salvation, this assurance can and should grow, deepen and mature. The marks, properly used, can be a major help in this area.

The marks, however, have sometimes been misused. There are some Christian groups who use the marks in a way that hinders full assurance of faith. While the Bible is clear that believers have a responsibility to examine themselves (Psa. 139:23, 24; Lam. 3:40; 1 Cor. 11:28; 2 Cor. 13:5), the purpose of such examination is not to leave true Christians in despair. Instead, it should lead to more consistent faith in and repentance towards Christ, the one upon whose merits believers must rely totally for salvation. When we look into our own hearts, who does not find reason for despair? Yet the true Christian will find evidences of life for which to be grateful, and in the process develop an earnest desire for greater growth in grace.

Remember that the new birth makes us new, but not yet perfect. Moral perfection is our desire, but its fulfilment lies in the future, in heaven and in the eternal state. A new Christian who had a foul mouth before conversion finds that the Lord cleans up his speech. Yet, he may be surprised one day, in the heat of the moment, to hear the old words come from his mouth. He may wonder, 'Am I really born again?' But what is the difference between his past and his present? In the past, those words flew at will from his lips and were truly expressive of his heart. But now, the new convert grieves over his words; he is deeply saddened by the continuation of indwelling sin. He longs to be done with such things, longs to please the Lord and desires the perfection which he will know in heaven. What are the evidences of the new birth in this case? A heart that grieves over sin and desires to please the Lord. This is a renewed heart. These marks are present because new life in Christ is present.

Another use of the marks of a Christian

There is another important use of the marks of a Christian. To a large extent, Jonathan Edwards' well-known book *The Religious Affections* was written to distinguish a true profession of faith from that which is false, especially, though certainly not exclusively, in times of revival. Times of revival in the church are a great blessing from the Lord for which we should earnestly long and pray. However, they often bring to the fore leaders who spread spiritual confusion in the church. Distinguishing the true from the false at such times is an important use of the marks of a Christian, which also are marks of true revival.

The marks of a Christian

There are many passages in the Bible to which a believer can and should turn in order to examine himself for evidences of life and, also, for areas of needed growth in grace. One such place is Galatians 5:22–24, the description of the fruit of the Spirit. Another is Matthew 5:3–11, the Beatitudes. Yet another is 1 John. Throughout this letter, written by the same John who wrote the Gospel bearing his name, there are clear marks that should be found in a Christian, such as living out the truth (1:6; 2:29; 3:7, 10), walking in the light (1:7; 2:6), obeying the Lord's commands (2:3, 5; 3:22, 24; 5:2, 3), loving fellow believers (2:10; 3:10–23; 4:7, 11, 21) and breaking radically with sin (2:17; 3:9, 22). Most importantly, throughout this little epistle there is emphasis upon believing in and confessing the Son of God. Once again, the Lord did not reveal these things in order to drive true believers to despair. On the contrary, John tells us that he wrote these things 'so that you may know that you have eternal life' (5:13). In addition to these places in Scripture, the Psalms have a wonderful ability to probe hearts and lead the true believer to a deeper understanding of his need of grace. In the Psalms we find, as Calvin said, 'an anatomy of all parts of the soul.'

Those who truly know the Lord will want their sin uncovered and will desire to believe and repent. Those who have 'temporal faith,' a temporary faith that is not saving, who build upon a false foundation, will not desire to have their life's foundation inspected. Surely, part of what it means to fear God is a willingness to say from the heart,

> Search me, O God, and know my heart! Try me and know my thoughts! And see if there be any grievous way in me, and lead me in the way everlasting! (Psa. 139:23, 24).

A life of humble obedience

Works do not save the Christian. Spirit-produced works, however, provide evidence of the new birth and spiritual resurrection. 'For we are his workmanship, created in Christ Jesus for good works, which God prepared beforehand, that we should walk in them' (Eph. 2:10). Edwards, in *The Religious Affections*, notes that true affections – the passions that motivate the soul – lead to a life that practises the Christian faith and lives out of communion with God. Hence, the twelfth and most important sign of true religious affections enumerated by Edwards is *practice*. 'Gracious and holy affections have their exercise and fruit in Christian practice.'[1] Holy practice is the Christian's universal desire, the 'business in which he is chiefly engaged'[2] and the thing in which the Christian perseveres to the end of his life, not just in certain seasons or at extraordinary times of heightened religious feelings. Titus 2:14 tells us that our Lord 'gave himself for us to redeem us from all lawlessness and to purify for himself a people for his own possession who are zealous for good works.' 'This fruit of holy practice is what every grace, and every discovery, and every individual thing, which belongs to Christian experience, has a direct tendency to.'[3] And, in this way, says Edwards, 'obedience, good works, good fruits, are to be taken, when given in Scripture as a sure evidence to our

---

[1] Jonathan Edwards, *The Religious Affections* (Edinburgh: Banner of Truth Trust, 1986), p. 308.

[2] Edwards, *The Religious Affections*, p. 308.

[3] Edwards, *The Religious Affections*, p. 321.

own consciences of a true principle of grace.'[1] A heart that is obedient to the Lord is 'the sign of signs' which 'confirms and crowns all other signs of godliness.' This is the proof of saving knowledge of God and of repentance, 'the proper evidence of saving faith.'[2] And, when assured Christians so live before the world, when 'the light of professors would so shine before men, ... others seeing their good works, [will] glorify their Father which is heaven.'[3]

The ground is Christ

The place and proper use of self-examination is a huge topic about which we have only been able to sketch a few important thoughts. Self-examination distinguishes the hypocrite from the true believer, divides true experience from false and is an aid to a greater subjective sense of assurance. Marks of grace will be present in every true believer, and self-examination should not destroy but, rather, strengthen the believer's subjective sense of assurance. The point, however, is not to stop with the marks but to allow the marks of grace to point us freshly to the Giver of grace. In the language of the Belgic Confession:[4]

> We would always be in doubt, tossed to and fro without any certainty, and our poor consciences would be continually vexed if they relied not on the merits of the suffering and death of our Saviour.

[1] Edwards, *The Religious Affections*, p. 345.
[2] Edwards, *The Religious Affections*, p. 365.
[3] Edwards, *The Religious Affections*, pp. 382.
[4] Article 24.

Further Reading

Where to Start

R. L. Dabney, *The Believer Born of Almighty Grace* in *Discussions of Robert Lewis Dabney* (Edinburgh: Banner of Truth Trust, 1982), vol. 1. pp. 482-495.

Arnold Dallimore, *George Whitefield,* 2 vols (Edinburgh: Banner of Truth Trust, 1970 and 1980).

J. C. Ryle, 'Regeneration' in *Knots Untied* (Edinburgh: Banner of Truth Trust, 2016), pp. 123-144.

Jonathan Edwards, 'Born Again,' in *The Works of Jonathan Edwards* (New Haven: Yale University Press), vol. 17, pp. 186-195.

Jonathan Edwards, *A Narrative of Surprising Conversions in Jonathan Edwards on Revival* (Edinburgh: Banner of Truth Trust, 2014).

C. H. Spurgeon, 'Regeneration' in *The New Park Street Pulpit* (Pasadena, Texas: Pilgrim Publications, 1975), pp. 185-192.

George Whitefield, 'On Regeneration' in *The Sermons of George Whitefield* (Wheaton: Crossway, 2012), pp. 275-287.

In More Detail

James Buchanan, *The Office and Word of the Holy Spirit* (Edinburgh: Banner of Truth Trust, 1984).

Jonathan Edwards, 'A Divine and Supernatural Light' in *The Works of Jonathan Edwards* (Edinburgh: Banner of Truth Trust), vol. 2, pp. 12-17.

Sinclair B. Ferguson, *The Holy Spirit* (Downers Grove, IL.: InterVarsity Press, 1996).

John Murray, *Redemption Accomplished and Applied* (Edinburgh: Banner of Truth Trust, 2016).

John Murray, 'Regeneration' in *Collected Writings of John Murray* (Edinburgh: Banner of Truth Trust, 1977), vol. 1.

George Smeaton, *The Doctrine of the Holy Spirit* (Edinburgh: Banner of Truth Trust, 2016).

C. R. Vaughan *Gifts of the Holy Spirit* (Edinburgh: Banner of Truth Trust, 1984).

The Bigger Picture

Herman Bavinck, 'The Order of Salvation,' *Reformed Dogmatics* (Grand Rapids: Baker, 2006), vol. 3, pp. 485-595. And, 'Calling and Regeneration,' *Reformed Dogmatics*, vol. 4, pp. 29-95.

Herman Bavinck, *Saved By Grace: The Holy Spirit's Work in Calling and Regeneration* (Grand Rapids: Reformation Heritage Books, 2008).

Thomas Boston, *Human Nature in Its Fourfold State* (Edinburgh: Banner of Truth Trust, 2015).

Wilhelmus à Brakel, 'Regeneration', *The Christian's Reasonable Service*, vol. 2 (Ligonier, PA: Soli Deo Gloria, 1993).

John Calvin, 'The Way in Which We Receive the Grace of Christ: What Benefits Come to Us from It, and What Effects Follow', *Institutes of the Christian Religion*, Book Three (Philadelphia: Westminster Press, 1960)

Stephen Charnock, 'The Necessity, the Nature, the Efficient, and the Instrument of Regeneration' in *The Works of Stephen Charnock* (Edinburgh: Banner of Truth Trust, 2010), vol. 3, pp. 7-385.

Jonathan Edwards, 'God Glorified in Man's Dependence' in *The Works of Jonathan Edwards* (Edinburgh: Banner of Truth Trust, 1974), vol. 2, pp. 3-7.

Jonathan Edwards, *A Treatise Concerning Religious Affections* (Edinburgh: Banner of Truth Trust, 2007)

Thomas Goodwin, *The Work of the Holy Spirit* (Edinburgh: Banner of Truth Trust, 1979)

G. H. Kersten, 'Calling' and 'Regeneration' in *Reformed Dogmatics* (Grand Rapids: Netherlands Reformed Publishing), vol. 2, pp. 364-393.

John Owen, *Discourse on the Holy Spirit* in *Works of John Owen*, vol. 3 (Edinburgh: Banner of Truth Trust, 2009)

Peter Van Mastricht *A Treatise on Regeneration* (Morgan, Pa.: Soli Deo Gloria, 2002).

Geerhardus Vos, 'Regeneration and Calling', *Reformed Dogmatics* (Bellingham, Wa., Lexham Press), vol. 4, pp. 29-57.

Banner Mini-Guides